One Truth, many lies

By Erik Rottmann

CONCORDIA PUBLISHING HOUSE · SAINT LOUIS

Written by Erik Rottmann

Edited by Mark S. Sengele

Unless otherwise indicated, Scripture quotations are from the ESV Bible® (The Holy Bible, English Standard Version®), copyright © 2001 by Crossway Bibles, a publishing ministry of Good News Publishers. Used by permission. All rights reserved.

Scripture quotations marked NIV are taken from the Holy Bible, New International Version®. NIV®. Copyright © 1973, 1978, 1984 by Biblica, Inc.™ Used by permission of Zondervan. All rights reserved.

Quotations from the Lutheran Confessions in this publication are from Concordia: The Lutheran Confessions, second edition; edited by Paul McCain, et al., copyright © 2006 Concordia Publishing House. All rights reserved.

Quotations from vols. 1, 3, 13, 24, and 28 of Luther's Works, American Edition, © 1958, 1961, 1956, 1961, 1973, respectively, by Concordia Publishing House, all rights reserved.

Quotation from vol. 52 of Luther's Works, American Edition, © 1974 Fortress Press. Used by permission of the publisher.

Material with the abbreviation LSB is from Lutheran Service Book, copyright © 2006 Concordia Publishing House. All rights reserved.

The quotation from C. F. W. Walther in Lesson 11 is taken from The Proper Distinction Between Law and Gospel, copyright © 1929, 1986 Concordia Publishing House. All rights reserved.

Cover art © Anette Linnea Rasmussen/Shutterstock, Inc.

This publication may be available in braille, in large print, or on cassette tape for the visually impaired. Please allow 8 to 12 weeks for delivery. Write to Lutheran Blind Mission, 7550 Watson Rd., St. Louis, MO 63119-4409; call toll-free 1-888-215-2455; or visit the Web site: www.blindmission.org.

Your comments and suggestions concerning this material are appreciated. Please write to Concordia Publishing House, 3558 S. Jefferson Avenue, St. Louis, MO 63118-3968.

Manufactured in the United States of America

1 2 3 4 5 6 7 8 9 10   20 19 18 17 16 15 14 13 12 11

Table of Contents

About this Book

When St. Paul wrote, "There must be factions among you" (1 Corinthians 11:19), the Greek word he used for "factions" is *haireseis*, or "heresies." In the singular, *hairesis* can mean "selection" or "division" or "faction." In Greek, *heresy* does not necessarily carry a negative meaning. In Christian history, the word has come to describe those teachings that depart from the main teachings of God's Word and the ancient creeds (Apostles', Nicene, and Athanasian) that summarize God's Word.

Heresies are ancient, but not obsolete! Oxford University's Alister McGrath notes that many heresies are today embraced as expressions of individuality and religious freedom. This rising interest in heresy has motivated *One Truth, Many Lies*.

While *all* departures from God's Word carry serious consequences, some departures—some heresies—are more serious than others. For example:

A Christian might reject the words of Jesus concerning Holy Communion, "This is My body. . . . This is My blood" (Matthew 26:26, 28). While there are serious consequences for this departure from the Word of God (1 Corinthians 11:30), a Christian who rejects these words does not necessarily cease to be Christian.

By comparison, no one remains Christian who rejects that God is triune: Father, Son, and Holy Spirit (Matthew 28:19). If you reject the Trinity, you reject the God of the Christians, and you divide yourself—you *heresy* yourself, so to speak—away from the life and salvation that God gives to His Christians.

Which heresies will completely separate you from the Christian faith? The Athanasian Creed draws these two lines in the sand:

Whoever desires to be saved must, above all, hold the catholic faith. Whoever does not keep it whole and undefiled will without doubt perish eternally. And the catholic faith is this, that we worship one God in Trinity and Trinity in Unity, neither confusing the persons nor dividing the substance. . . .

It is also necessary for everlasting salvation that one faithfully believe the incarnation of our Lord Jesus Christ. Therefore, it is the right faith that we believe and confess that our Lord Jesus Christ, the Son of God, is at the same time both God and man. (*LSB*, pp. 319–20)

Because the most consequential heresies have to do with the Trinity and the two natures of Christ, *One Truth, Many Lies* follows the three-part pattern of the Apostles' Creed. Unit 1 treats those heresies that have to do with who God is and what He has said. Unit 2 treats the heresies specific to Jesus Christ, our Lord. Unit 3 deals with heresies pertaining to the Third Article of the Creed: the work of the Holy Spirit, the gift of salvation, the ministry of the Church, and the resurrection of the dead.

Preparing to Teach

As you prepare to teach, please note the following themes:

1. **The Continual Return to God's Word**
The main purpose of this study is to help you and your class to emulate the Christians in Acts 17:11, who were "examining the Scriptures daily to see if these things were so." This study will help you and your class to listen more carefully to the Word of God, to "grow in the grace and knowledge of our Lord and Savior Jesus Christ" (2 Peter 3:18), and "to make a defense to anyone who asks you for a reason for the hope that is in you" (1 Peter 3:15).

2. **The Deepening Understanding of the Lutheran Faith, Drawn Exclusively from the Word** You can gain a greater understanding of what you believe by understanding more clearly what you do *not* believe and why. When the earliest Lutherans confessed their faith, they also specified what they did not believe. Major heretics were frequently mentioned. For example, the Lutherans stated in their Augsburg Confession (1530):

> **Our churches teach that since the fall of Adam [Romans 5:12], all who are naturally born are born with sin [Psalm 51:5], that is without the fear of God, without trust in God, and with the inclination to sin. (Augsburg Confession, Article II, paragraph 1)**

Then the Lutherans immediately emphasized their point by condemning the followers of the ancient heretic Pelagius: "Our churches condemn the Pelagians and others who deny that original depravity is sin" (Augsburg Confession, Article II, paragraph 1).

3. **Speaking to Other People** Many Lutherans have friends or family members, both Christian and unbeliever, who hold strange opinions about Christianity. All Lutherans have daily opportunities to speak the faith to others. Knowledge of major heresies, past and present, is an important tool for profitable conversations.

The following considerations may be helpful as you prepare to teach:

Materials: Each session has a Participant Page that may be reproduced for each participant. Bibles will be necessary, and participants may wish to have a pen or pencil for notes. According to your teaching style, you might also wish to use newsprint and markers, a whiteboard, or the like.

Schedule: Do not feel compelled to complete a given session within a certain time frame. If a particular session's materials have not yet been covered by the end of your allotted time, feel free to continue the same conversation and session materials during the next gathering of the class. If you complete a session before the class time has expired, feel free to begin introducing the next session.

The Word! The Word! The Word! As each heresy is examined, everyone should continually bear in mind the main purpose of *One Truth, Many Lies*, which is to study God's Word. Each class session will examine several Bible passages, which should be examined beforehand by the instructor.

Regular Review: It might be helpful for each class session to review the introductory material of the respective unit. This will help the participants to understand how each heresy fits within a larger historical context.

Much More Could Be Said!

In this Bible study, I have only sought to (1) distill each heresy down to a couple of main points, and (2) explain how these points still threaten the Christian faith today.

Most Bible studies are necessarily brief, and this one is no exception. Brevity comes at a cost, and two regrets are noted: First, the heresies studied here are only a few that have occurred in the history of the Church. These few were selected because of the temptation each still poses, but many other heresies certainly could have been included. Second, brevity requires oversimplification, and over-simplification opens the door to misrepresen-tation. I have explained only enough details of each heresy to make my intended point.

Oversimplification also means that the solution to these heresies looks easy. It should be borne in mind that each of these her-esies posed serious threats to the Church, often encompassing many decades, and the answers that were finally given to these her-esies came as a result of hard labor.

Section One

First Article

**I believe in God,
the Father Almighty,
Maker of heaven and earth.**

What does this mean?

I believe that God has made me and all creatures; that He has given me my body and soul, eyes, ears, and all my members, my reason and all my senses, and still takes care of them.

He also gives me clothing and shoes, food and drink, house and home, wife and children, land, animals, and all I have. He richly and daily provides me with all that I need to support this body and life.

He defends me against all danger and guards and protects me from all evil.

All this He does only out of fatherly, divine goodness and mercy, without any merit or worthiness in me. For all this it is my duty to thank and praise, serve and obey Him.

This is most certainly true.

1

Humans

Lesson Focus

Because all people are born with the deadly disease of sin, heresy is not merely the error into which another person might fall. Because it naturally appeals to our inherited disease of sin, heresy lurks in every Christian heart and mind. Heresy is *your* temptation.

Historical Context

Genesis 3:6 marks the first and the worst heresy: "When the woman saw that the tree was good for food, and that it was a delight to the eyes, and that the tree was to be desired to make one wise, she took of its fruit and ate, and she also gave some to her husband who was with her, and he ate."

Two things happened in this heresy that are essential for understanding all heresies. First, Adam and Eve chose between what God said and what seemed reasonable. On the one hand, God clearly warned, "In the day that you eat of it you shall surely die" (Genesis 2:17). On the other hand, the fruit "was a delight to the eyes." Following their senses rather than the Word of God, Adam and Eve fell into heresy before they even pressed the fruit to their lips! In so doing, Adam and Eve set the pattern all heretics have followed since.

Second, sin and death pierced Adam, Eve, and all their descendants. Paul explains the consequence of the first heresy: "Death spread to all men. . . . One trespass led to condemnation for all" (Romans 5:12, 18). Just as apples produce apples and monkeys produce monkeys, people capable of heresy produce people capable of heresy. Each of us has been born embedded with the same sin and corruption that destroyed Adam and Eve. Because of this, your study of heresy is not merely a study of what others have said and done. You are also studying your own capabilities.

Distribute copies of Participant Page 1 if desired. Read aloud the Historical Context, above, and the Message from Martin Luther. Then pray responsively the Opening Prayer.

A Message from Martin Luther

Eve agrees with Satan when he charges God with lying, and, as it were, strikes God in the face with his fists. . . . She joins with Satan in despising God and denying the Word of God, and she believes the father of lies rather than the Word of God.

Let these events be a warning for us that we may learn what man is. For if this happened when nature was still perfect, what do we think will happen to us now? (Luther's Works, American Edition, Volume 1, page 156)

Opening Prayer

L: Let Your steadfast love come to me, O Lord,

P: Your salvation according to Your promise;

L: Then shall I have an answer for him who taunts me,

P: For I trust in Your word. (Psalm 119:41–42)

L: Forever, O Lord, Your word is firmly fixed in the heavens.

P: Your faithfulness endures to all generations. (Psalm 119:89–90a)

Inherited Sin

What do the following verses say about the inherited disease of sin?

Genesis 6:5—"Every intention of the thoughts of his [humanity's] heart was only evil continually."

Romans 8:7—"The mind that is set on the flesh is hostile to God."

Ephesians 4:22—"Your old self . . . is corrupt through deceitful desires."

Pointing to verses such as these, our Lutheran forefathers confessed, "Christians should regard and recognize the actual transgression of God's commandments as sin; but sin is also that horrible, dreadful hereditary sickness by which the entire human nature is corrupted" (Solid Declaration of the Formula of Concord, Article I, paragraph 5).

Use the following verses to determine whether this statement is true or false: apart from God's Word, it is impossible for us to know about our inherited disease of sin and the countless ways this disease becomes evident in our lives.

Psalm 19:12—"Who can discern his errors? Declare me innocent from hidden faults."

Psalm 40:12—"Evils have encompassed me beyond number; . . . they are more than the hairs of my head."

Romans 7:7—"If it had not been for the law, I would not have known sin."

Each of these verses shows how sin goes far beyond what we knowingly say or do. We need God's Scriptures to declare to us the seriousness of sin because we simply could not otherwise recognize or believe it.

What does Romans 7:15–20 say about each Christian's ongoing capability to fall into any sort of heresy? "Nothing good dwells in me, that is, in my flesh. . . . Sin dwells within me" (vv. 18, 20). Because the disease never goes away, all Christians are continually capable of committing the worst sorts of sin, including heresy and blasphemy. You might not be able to draw such a conclusion simply by looking into a mirror, but your inherited disease of sin indicates that you—like all other people—personally have the capacity for any sort of evil.

The Power of the Word

According to Ephesians 2:1–5 and Colossians 1:13–14, what is God's antidote for our inherited disease of sin? Jesus Christ, the crucified and resurrected Son of God, richly and completely forgives all your sin—not merely your acts of sin, but your disease of sin! "When we were dead in our trespasses, [God] made us alive together with Christ" (Ephesians 2:5). With these words, Paul wants you to know that Jesus' death and resurrection are not merely your source of life some day in the future, when God raises you from the dead. Jesus' death and resurrection are your source of life each and every day, powerfully overcoming the disease of sin for you on a daily basis. Because "He has delivered us from the domain of darkness . . . , we have redemption, the forgiveness of sins" (Colossians 1:13–14).

What do the following verses say about God's ongoing protection of your heart and mind so that you do not fall into heresy?

Romans 1:16—The Gospel, that is, the Good News of Jesus Christ's death and resurrection for the forgiveness of your sins, is the "power of God." The Greek word for power, *dunamis*, is the word from which we get the word *dynamite*. God's Gospel is dynamite, continually exploding sin and death for you!

1 Corinthians 1:18—The cross is "the power of God," with the same word for "power" as in Romans 1:16.

1 Thessalonians 2:13—God's Word is "at work in you believers." In the same way that yeast works in dough, so God's Word actively works in you, expanding and growing and protecting you from the harmful effects the disease of sin exerts on you.

How might the preceding verses influence the way you think about God's Third Commandment, "Remember the Sabbath Day, to keep it holy" (Exodus 20:8), and such verses as 1 Timothy 4:13 and Hebrews 10:25? That is why each Christian needs a regular supply of God's Word, preached and administered in the Sacraments. Just like a cancer patient needs regular chemotherapy to combat his or her tumor, Christians need regular worship to combat the disease of sin! This is why Paul exhorts Timothy to devote himself to "the public reading of Scripture" (1 Timothy 4:13) and why the Book of Hebrews calls upon you not to neglect meeting together (Hebrews 10:25) around God's Word and Sacraments.

Deliver Us from Evil

What warnings are written in 2 Peter 2:1–2, 17–18? In addition to each Christian's inborn capacity for heresy, "There will be false teachers among you, who will secretly bring in destructive heresies" (v. 1). Such false teachers gain a following because they appeal to "passions of the flesh" (v. 18). Stated another way, false teachers succeed because they tell people things they want to hear.

What protection against heresy does God promise to you in the following verses?

John 10:1–5—"The sheep hear his voice" (v. 3). God's Word is the voice of Jesus. When you have Jesus' voice in your ears and when you have learned well the sound of His voice, it will be very difficult for you to be led astray by false shepherds!

Philippians 4:7—God's Word brings you peace—a peace that cannot be understood or described or inwardly felt. However, this peace actively and attentively "will guard your hearts and your minds in Christ Jesus" so that heresy will exert no power over you.

Revelation 2:16b—Jesus promises to "war against them with the sword of [His] mouth," which is the Word of God. The Scriptures are more than a defense for you. The Scriptures are the words of God, which actively wage war in order to keep you in the true faith.

Closing Prayer

Guard and protect us, dear Lord Jesus! Draw us ever closer to the Scriptures, the words You have written, that these words may keep us safe from the temptations of the evil one, the lures of the unbelieving world, and the inclinations of our own hearts. By the power of Your Word and Spirit, keep us firm and unwavering in the true faith unto life everlasting. Amen.

1

Humans

A Message from Martin Luther

Eve agrees with Satan when he charges God with lying, and, as it were, strikes God in the face with his fists. . . . She joins with Satan in despising God and denying the Word of God, and she believes the father of lies rather than the Word of God.

Let these events be a warning for us that we may learn what man is. For if this happened when nature was still perfect, what do we think will happen to us now? (Luther's Works, American Edition, Volume 1, page 156)

Opening Prayer

L: Let Your steadfast love come to me, O Lord,

P: Your salvation according to Your promise;

L: Then shall I have an answer for him who taunts me,

P: For I trust in Your word. (Psalm 119:41–42)

L: Forever, O Lord, Your word is firmly fixed in the heavens.

P: Your faithfulness endures to all generations.
(Psalm 119:89–90a)

Inherited Sin

What do the following verses say about the inherited disease of sin?

Genesis 6:5

Romans 8:7

Ephesians 4:22

Use the following verses to determine whether this statement is true or false: apart from God's Word, it is impossible for us to know about our inherited disease of sin and the countless ways this disease becomes evident in our lives.

Psalm 19:12

Psalm 40:12

Romans 7:7

What does **Romans 7:15–20** say about each Christian's ongoing capability to fall into any sort of heresy?

The Power of the Word

According to **Ephesians 2:1–5** and **Colossians 1:13–14**, what is God's antidote for our inherited disease of sin?

What do the following verses say about God's ongoing protection of your heart and mind, so that you do not fall into heresy?

Romans 1:16

1 Corinthians 1:18

1 Thessalonians 2:13

How might the preceding verses influence the way you think about God's Third Commandment, "Remember the Sabbath Day, to keep it holy" (**Exodus 20:8**), and such verses as **1 Timothy 4:13** and **Hebrews 10:25**?

Deliver Us from Evil

What warnings are written in **2 Peter 2:1–2, 17–18**?

What protection against heresy does God promise to you in the following verses?

John 10:1–5

Philippians 4:7

Revelation 2:16b

2

Manichaeans

Lesson Focus

Manichaeans believed that evil is not a foreign intrusion into the creation, but that evil has been in conflict with good from eternity. This teaching appeals to our inherited disease of sin because it allows us to blame our sin on someone or something other than ourselves.

Historical Context

In the third century AD, a Persian named Mani founded a new religion by claiming that he was able to receive special revelations from God. Mani not only called himself the last and greatest of the prophets, but also the Paraclete whom Jesus had promised to send.

Mani's teachings were a hodgepodge of ideas he gathered from various other religions, including Christianity. Mani used many biblical words and terms (e.g., *Paraclete*), which he redefined for his own use. Many Christians were deceived by his teachings. The most famous Manichaean, who later repented of the heresy, was Augustine of Hippo.

Manichaeans taught a very strict lifestyle that incorporated vegetarianism, obligatory prayer, fasting, and ceremonial purifications. Manichaeans were forbidden to engage in business, drink alcohol, own property, or settle anywhere permanently.

While New Manichaeans have a small following today, some Manichaean teachings appeal very well to each person's inherited disease of sin. For example, Manichaeans teach that evil has been in eternal conflict with good, and that it is not merely a foreign entrance into God's good and perfect creation. The strict Manichaean lifestyle was aimed toward limiting and containing the power of evil. However, because humans are seen as merely participants in a greater cosmic struggle, no one is individually responsible for his or her own sin. "The devil made me do it," so to speak.

Distribute copies of Participant Page 2 if desired. Read aloud the Historical Context, above, and the Message from the Lutheran Confessions. Then pray responsively the Opening Prayer.

A Message from the Lutheran Confessions

We reject . . . the ideas of the Manichaeans, who taught that everything that happens must happen and cannot happen otherwise; everything that a person does, even in outward things, he does by compulsion; he is forced to do evil works and deeds, such as inchastity, robbery, murder, theft, and the like. (Epitome of the Formula of Concord, Article II, paragraph 8)

Opening Prayer

L: God is light, and in Him is no darkness at all.

P: If we say we have fellowship with Him while we walk in darkness, we lie and do not practice the truth.

L: But if we walk in the light, as He is in the light, we have fellowship with one another,

P: And the blood of Jesus His Son cleanses us from all sin. (1 John 1:5b–7)

L: Forever, O Lord, Your word is firmly fixed in the heavens.

P: Your faithfulness endures to all generations. (Psalm 119:89–90a)

Prehistory Perfection

In what way do the following verses help you understand that evil has not existed from eternity, contrary to the Manichaean claim?

John 1:1–3—John states that in the beginning, there was nothing but God. Everything else that exists, therefore, must have come into the world sometime after the beginning. God is not evil, so evil cannot be eternal. Only God is eternal!

Genesis 1:31—"God saw *everything* that He had made, and behold, it was very good" (emphasis added). This verse, along with the previously cited passage from John 1, requires us to believe that God is the source of everything good, and *only* good things. Evil is foreign to the creation, foreign to God, and by no means eternal.

If evil existed from eternity, then God must be the source of evil. How do these verses answer such false thinking?

Leviticus 19:2 and Isaiah 6:1–7—God is holy, which means that there is no shade of unholiness or evil within Him at all.

Psalm 5:4–5—More than not being the source of evil, God feels no sense of toleration toward evil. God does not wink at sin as if sin were not a problem, and He hates evildoers.

James 1:13—God also does not entice His dear people with evil; "He Himself tempts no one."

According to Genesis 3:1–5 and John 8:44, what role did the serpent/Satan play in introducing evil into the world? The serpent challenged God's Word and threw a seed of doubt into Eve's mind. By this act, and by every effort since, Satan has been actively murdering those whom God created. By enticing to sin, Satan opens the door to death.

Despite the serpent's role in destroying the creation, who ultimately is held responsible for sin entering the world? See Romans 5:12. Paul hangs the responsibility for sin—and for the entry of evil into the world—around Adam's neck. It is almost as if Paul says, "Forget the false idea of evil being eternal! Sin came into the world through Adam, and with sin comes death. There is no evil greater than death."

We're No Angels!

If evil existed from eternity, as the Manichaeans claimed, what does this say about your personal responsibility for the wrong things you say and do? If evil existed from eternity, then you are simply a helpless victim. You cannot be held ultimately responsible for the wrong things you say and do. Can a man born blind be blamed for his blindness? If evil existed from eternity, then you have no escape from it.

Is there a sense in which you can blame Adam or your parents for your sin? See Psalm 51:5 and Job 14:4. Sure! Sin was passed to you from your parents. In the same way that dogs give birth to dogs and cats give birth to cats, sinful people give birth to sinful people. After all, how can something pure come forth from that which is impure?

How does Paul ensure your personal blame and responsibility for your sin in Romans 3:23 and 5:12–14? Not only have you been born with the inherited disease of sin, but you have also been actively adding to your guilt by sinning from the moment of your birth. "*All* have sinned" (Romans 3:23, emphasis added). "Death spread to all men because all sinned" (Romans 5:12).

Return to James 1:13–15. What do these verses say about each person's "process" of falling into sin? In a manner very much like what took place in the Garden of Eden, each individual sins when enticed away—not by force!—by his or her own evil desires. Then a birth process takes place: "Desire when it has conceived gives birth to sin, and sin when it is fully grown brings forth death" (v. 15).

Closing Prayer

Teach us to know our sin aright, O heavenly Father, for where there is no sin, there is no need for redemption. By the power of Your Word and Spirit, enable us to acknowledge our personal guilt, to confess our sin, and to believe firmly in the eternal forgiveness that Your Son, Jesus, has earned for all people by His death and resurrection. Amen.

2

Manichaeans

A Message from the Lutheran Confessions

We reject . . . the ideas of the Manichaeans, who taught that everything that happens must happen and cannot happen otherwise; everything that a person does, even in outward things, he does by compulsion; he is forced to do evil works and deeds, such as inchastity, robbery, murder, theft, and the like. (Epitome of the Formula of Concord, Article II, paragraph 8)

Opening Prayer

L: God is light, and in Him is no darkness at all.

P: If we say we have fellowship with Him while we walk in darkness, we lie and do not practice the truth.

L: But if we walk in the light, as He is in the light, we have fellowship with one another,

P: And the blood of Jesus His Son cleanses us from all sin. (1 John 1:5b–7)

L: Forever, O Lord, Your word is firmly fixed in the heavens.

P: Your faithfulness endures to all generations. (Psalm 119:89–90a)

Prehistory Perfection

In what way do the following verses help you understand that evil has *not* existed from eternity, contrary to the Manichaean claim?

John 1:1–3

Genesis 1:31

If evil existed from eternity, then God must be the source of evil. How do these verses answer such false thinking?

Leviticus 19:2 and **Isaiah 6:1–7**

Psalm 5:4–5

James 1:13

According to **Genesis 3:1–5** and **John 8:44**, what role did the serpent/Satan play in introducing evil into the world?

Despite the serpent's role in destroying the creation, who is held ultimately responsible for sin's entry into the world? See **Romans 5:12**.

We're No Angels!

If evil existed from eternity, as the Manichaeans claimed, what does this say about your personal responsibility for the wrong things you say and do?

Is there a sense in which you can blame Adam or your parents for your sin? See **Psalm 51:5** and **Job 14:4**.

How does Paul ensure your personal blame and responsibility for your sin in **Romans 3:23** and **5:12–14**?

Return to **James 1:13–15**. What do these verses say about each person's "process" of falling into sin?

MANICHAEANS   *19*

3

Arians

Lesson Focus

Arius famously taught, "There was a time when the Son was not." Arius presupposed that God the Father is totally and utterly inaccessible and God the Son had to be created as an intermediary or a go-between. This teaching appeals to our inherited disease of sin because it allows us to believe that God, rather than sin, is responsible for the seeming gulf we feel between Him and us.

Historical Context

Arius (d. 336 AD) is a great example of someone whose presuppositions led him away from the Christian faith. Arius allowed his thoughts to be guided and preformed by a philosophy called Neoplatonism, which taught that all material things are essentially evil and only purely spiritual things are good. (This is called "dualism.") Motivated by dualism, Arius reasoned that because God is purely spirit (good), it would be impossible for God to become incarnate, that is, to have a material (evil) human body.

Arius then read the Bible with this simple line of thinking in mind: The eternal God is incapable of entering into human history (Neoplatonism); God the Son entered human history in the person of Jesus, Mary's human Son (Bible); therefore, God the Son must not be eternal. God the Son had to be inferior to God the Father because the Son was able to bridge the gap between the Father and the creation. This is why Arius insisted, "There was a time when the Son was not."

Arius denied the Trinity, and that *is* heresy. Arius denied the divinity of Christ, and that is *also* heresy. The main point here, though, is how Arius arrived at his heresy. Arius allowed his thought process to be preformed and guided by human philosophy, not by God's Word. Arianism tempts us to think that reason and philosophy can teach us about God, rather than learning about Him from His Word alone.

Distribute copies of Participant Page 3 if desired. Read aloud the Historical Context, above, and the Message from the Lutheran Confessions. Then pray responsively the Opening Prayer.

A Message from the Lutheran Confessions

The New Arians teach that Christ is not true, essential, natural God, of one eternal divine essence with God the Father. They say He is only adorned with divine majesty inferior to, and beside, God the Father. (Solid Declaration of the Formula of Concord, Article XII, paragraph 36)

Opening Prayer

L: In the beginning was the Word, and the Word was with God, and the Word was God.

P: He was in the beginning with God.

L: All things were made through Him,

P: And without Him was not any thing made that was made. (John 1:1–3)

L: Forever, O LORD, Your word is firmly fixed in the heavens.

P: Your faithfulness endures to all generations. (Psalm 119:89–90a)

God Saw It Was . . .

Review the story of creation in Genesis 1–2. After each physical thing was created, what repeated sentence emphasized its goodness? Throughout the story of creation, again and again it is stated, "And God saw that it was good." Thus, the very beginning of the Scriptures defies the basic idea of dualism, that matter is evil and only spiritual things are good. God created all things perfectly, and all things are specifically called "good."

Dualism caused Arius to assume that God must remain distant from His creation. How does Genesis 3:8 contradict such an assumption? At one time, God walked together with Adam and Even "in the cool of the day." God did not wish to remain separate and independent of His creation, but from the very beginning, God was face-to-face with His creatures. Only the intrusion of sin caused a separation between man and God.

The Eternity of the Son

What answer does John 1:1–14 give to the Arian claim "There was a time when the Son was not"? Speaking about God's Son, Jesus, John famously wrote, "In the beginning was the Word, and the Word was with God, and the Word was God" (v. 1). The Jehovah's Witnesses, modern-day Arians, cannot abide these words. That is why their "Bible" has mistranslated John 1:1 to read, "and the Word was a God."

What help do Colossians 1:18–19 and 2:9 provide in thinking about who Jesus, God the Son, is? Paul emphasizes that Jesus is not a "subgod" or lesser god than the Father, but rather, in Jesus "*is* the beginning" (1:18, emphasis added). Additionally, "In Him [Jesus] all the fullness of God was pleased to dwell" (v. 19). Again, "In Him [Jesus] the whole fullness of deity dwells bodily" (2:9). That is to say, there is no part of God that remained separated or distant from the physical human body. Everything that is God united and became one with human flesh in Jesus.

In what way do John 20:20 and Luke 24:37–39 show you that Jesus does not wish to escape or be separated from His own human body? Dualism suggests that after Jesus rose from the dead, He would no longer wish to possess a human body. After all, if the physical body were evil, then Jesus would have wanted to escape His body as soon as possible. But Jesus demonstrates the created goodness of the human body by keeping His body after the resurrection. "A spirit does not have flesh and bones as you see that I have" (Luke 24:39).

Human Philosophy Takes Prisoners!

If Arian dualism is correct, then who is to blame for our separation from God? According to dualism, human sin cannot be the cause of our separation from God. Sin is entirely inconsequential on account of the unbridgeable gulf that already exists between the spiritual God and physical humanity. Under Arian thinking, Christ's crucifixion ultimately becomes useless because even though sin is forgiven, we still have a separation from God.

Dualism is a purely human idea, dreamed up by a person and without any thought toward God's Scriptures. What does Paul say in Colossians 2:8 about such types of thinking? Paul warns you that human philosophy will take you captive! "See to it that no one takes you captive by philosophy and empty deceit, according to human tradition, according to the elemental spirits of the world, and not according to Christ."

What does Paul famously say in 1 Corinthians 1:18–25 about the "wisdom" of human ideas such as dualism? God has made all the highest wisdom of humanity into foolishness. He did this so that people would be saved not on the basis of their philosophical ideas, but by "the word of the cross" (v. 18). When human thinking takes the driver's seat, as it did with Arius, then the true wisdom—the wisdom of the cross—is lost.

Closing Prayer

Your Word, O Lord, Your Word alone! By the power of Your Word and Spirit, keep our hearts and minds focused upon what You have written in Your Scriptures, so that we may not be attracted by our own human opinions or by the philosophies of the unbelieving world. Amen.

3

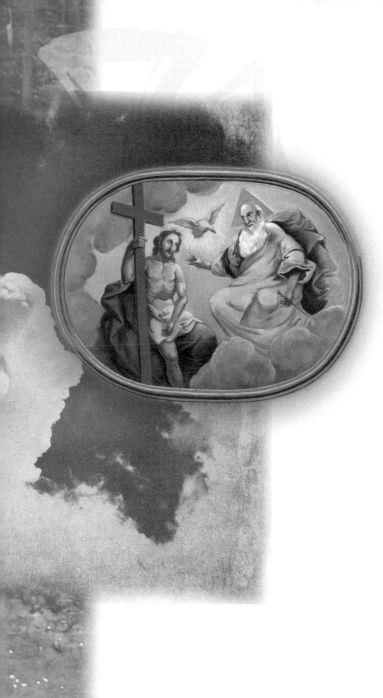

Arians

A Message from the Lutheran Confessions

The New Arians teach that Christ is not true, essential, natural God, of one eternal divine essence with God the Father. They say He is only adorned with divine majesty inferior to, and beside, God the Father. (Solid Declaration of the Formula of Concord, Article XII, paragraph 36)

Opening Prayer

L: In the beginning was the Word, and the Word was with God, and the Word was God.

P: He was in the beginning with God.

L: All things were made through Him,

P: And without Him was not any thing made that was made. (John 1:1–3)

L: Forever, O LORD, Your word is firmly fixed in the heavens.

P: Your faithfulness endures to all generations. (Psalm 119:89–90a)

God Saw It Was . . .

Review the story of creation in **Genesis 1–2**. After each physical thing was created, what repeated sentence emphasized its goodness?

Dualism caused Arius to assume that God must remain distant from His creation. How does **Genesis 3:8** contradict such an assumption?

The Eternity of the Son

What answer does **John 1:1–14** give to the Arian claim "There was a time when the Son was not"?

What help do **Colossians 1:18–19** and **2:9** provide in thinking about who Jesus, God the Son, is?

In what way do **John 20:20** and **Luke 24:37–39** show you that Jesus does not wish to escape or be separated from His own human body?

Human Philosophy Takes Prisoners!

If Arian dualism is correct, then who is to blame for our separation from God?

Dualism is a purely human idea, dreamed up by a person and without any thought toward God's Scriptures. What does Paul say in **Colossians 2:8** about such types of thinking?

What does Paul famously say in **1 Corinthians 1:18–25** about the "wisdom" of human ideas such as dualism?

4

Sabellians

Lesson Focus

Sabellius taught modalistic Monarchianism, which is the idea that the three persons of the Trinity are not distinct persons, but merely three phases, or modes, of one God. This teaching appeals to our inherited disease of sin because it uses reason and logic as a way of "solving" those teachings in the Scriptures that do not make sense to our human way of thinking.

Historical Context

Modalistic Monarchianism cropped up in several churches during the early part of the third century AD, including in Rome, where Sabellius led the movement. One particular feature of Sabellius's modalism was "patripassionism" (*patri* = Latin for "father"; *passion* = Latin for "suffering"). Basing itself on the idea that God the Son is merely a mode or phase of God the Father, patripassionism claims that God the Father therefore became incarnate, suffered, and died on the cross.

Modalistic Monarchianism is still alive and well today, especially in "oneness" church bodies. The United Pentecostal Church, for example, expressly denies the Trinity by claiming that the titles Father, Son, and Holy Spirit are only that—three different titles describing different modes or phases of God. (Like all others who deny the Trinity, the "oneness" church bodies should not be regarded as Christian, even though they may use the word *Christian* to describe themselves.)

While many Christians might find it easy to reject such denials of the Trinity, the underlying assumption in Sabellianism is a universal temptation. Sabellianism is built upon the very appealing idea that human reason or logic can "make sense" or "iron out" those things in God's Word that seem illogical or unreasonable. Stated another way, Sabellianism—like every other heresy—appeals to your brain, and not the Scriptures, as the ultimate source of your knowledge of God.

Distribute copies of Participant Page 4 if desired. Read aloud the Historical Context, above, and the Message from Martin Luther. Then pray responsively the Opening Prayer.

A Message from Martin Luther

While natural reason easily grasps that there is only one God, and many statements of the Bible substantiate this—and it is, of course, true—natural reason argues most violently against the notion that more than one person should be the same God.

That is why there arose the heretic, Sabellius, who says that Father, Son, and Holy Ghost are only one person. (Luther's Works, American Edition, Volume 52, page 48)

Opening Prayer

L: Behold, a voice from heaven said,

P: "This is My beloved Son, with whom I am well pleased." (Matthew 3:17)

L: When the fullness of time had come, God sent forth His Son . . . so that we might receive adoption as sons.

P: And because [we] are sons, God has sent the Spirit of His Son into our hearts, crying, "Abba! Father!" (Galatians 4:4a, 5b–6)

L: Forever, O Lord, Your word is firmly fixed in the heavens.

P: Your faithfulness endures to all generations. (Psalm 119:89–90a)

Three Persons in One God

According to the following verses, is God one or is God three?

Genesis 1:26—The words "Let Us make man" indicate the presence of more than one person of the Trinity at creation. This verse allows us to think that God might be more than one. However,

Deuteronomy 6:4—This is the creed, so to speak, of ancient Israel: "The Lord our God . . . is one." Contrary to most of the false and idolatrous religions all around Israel, which were polytheistic, Israel's God is one.

Isaiah 64:3–4—Isaiah proclaims that there is no God other than the one God who "did awesome things" by coming down on Mount Sinai and delivering the Ten Commandments to Israel. However,

Matthew 28:19—Jesus sends out His disciples, commanding them to baptize in the name of the triune God: the Father, Son, and Holy Spirit.

These verses are only a few examples of many verses that describe God as three and God as one. The doctrine of the Trinity holds all these verses, without attempting to reconcile the logical contradiction. Rather than trying to "solve" the mystery of the Trinity, the Christian faith simply holds and confesses the mystery, which it cannot fathom or comprehend.

What does Paul say in Romans 3:4 about human attempts to "iron out" or "solve" or "make sense" of the seemingly contradictory things that God says about Himself? Given the choice between (1) listening to God's Word and believing it (despite our inability fully to comprehend it) and (2) using human thinking and philosophy to explain or reconcile or "iron out" what God has said, Paul states, "Let God be true though every one were a liar."

When the prophet Job encountered things about God that he could not fully understand or explain, what did he wisely do? Briefly review God's speech in Job 38–39, and then read Job's response in 40:4–5. After listening to Job complain for a very long time about his situation, God spoke. God wanted to know what Job knew about being God, and God asked Job a great many questions about Job's power, strength, and ability to create. Job wisely chose to remain silent, knowing that God's knowledge and might far exceeded Job's own. In the same way, when we Christians encounter things in God's Word that we cannot comprehend or understand, it is best to remain silent rather than to attempt to give a human explanation to things that are divine.

For what does David pray in Psalm 119:18? David asks God miraculously to open his eyes, so that he may see and understand many things in God's Word. (The English translation is "law," but the Hebrew word is *torah*, which is better translated as "word.") With these words, David is saying that he cannot see or understand the wonderful things God says in the Scriptures unless God makes him able to do so.

Wisdom from Above

What do the following verses say about human ability to perceive and understand the mysteries of God?

Isaiah 55:8–9—Through Isaiah, God says that His thoughts and ways are far beyond the thoughts and ways of any human being. "As the heavens are higher than the earth, so are My ways higher than your ways and My thoughts than your thoughts" (v. 9).

1 Corinthians 2:14—With the illumination and help of the Holy Spirit, who speaks through the Scriptures, we humans cannot "accept the things of the Spirit of God." The teachings of the Scriptures, including the Trinity, appear as nothing but foolishness to those who do not believe.

James 3:14–17—Because of the inherited disease of sin, human thinking is more than "earthly" and "unspiritual." Natural human thinking is demonic, that is, in step with the way the devil and his demons do their thinking, rather than in step with God.

Why is it vitally important for you that the mysteries of God cannot be understood or perceived on the basis of human intellect and thinking? If God could be understood or perceived on the basis of human thinking, then those people with the highest intelligence or abilities at perception would be "better" Christians, while less intelligent people would be "lesser" Christians. By relying solely upon God's revelation and not upon the abilities of human reason, all people are equal in the eyes of God and, as Paul says, "no one may boast" (Ephesians 2:9).

Who Was That Crucified Man?

What do the following verses clearly state about the man who was crucified?

Mark 15:39—"Truly this man was the *Son* of God!" (emphasis added).

John 3:16—God the Father could not have been crucified because "God so loved the world, that He gave His only Son" to be crucified.

Galatians 4:4–5—As with John 3:16, "God sent forth His Son, born of woman."

Why is the death of God's Son a greater sacrifice than the death of God the Father, if such a death were even possible (as patripassionism claims)? Most parents can agree that they would much rather give up their own life rather than sacrifice the life of their child. Stated another way, most parents agree that the sacrifice of the child would be a much greater loss than the sacrifice of one's self. God the Father made the greater sacrifice—He suffered the greatest loss possible—by offering His Son on the cross for our sins.

Closing Prayer

O Father, Son, and Holy Spirit, You have written many things that I cannot fully grasp with my mind or reason my way through. By the power of Your Word and Spirit, grant me grace to hold the Christian faith unwaveringly, despite my inability to comprehend every detail of what You have revealed in Your Word. Amen.

4

Sabellians

A Message from Martin Luther

While natural reason easily grasps that there is only one God, and many statements of the Bible substantiate this—and it is, of course, true—natural reason argues most violently against the notion that more than one person should be the same God.

That is why there arose the heretic, Sabellius, who says that Father, Son, and Holy Ghost are only one person. (Luther's Works, American Edition, Volume 52, page 48)

Opening Prayer

L: Behold, a voice from heaven said,

P: "This is My beloved Son, with whom I am well pleased."
(Matthew 3:17)

L: When the fullness of time had come, God sent forth His Son . . . so that we might receive adoption as sons.

P: And because [we] are sons, God has sent the Spirit of His Son into our hearts, crying, "Abba! Father!"
(Galatians 4:4a, 5b–6)

L: Forever, O Lord, Your word is firmly fixed in the heavens.

P: Your faithfulness endures to all generations. (Psalm 119:89–90a)

Three Persons in One God

According to the following verses, is God one or is God three?

Genesis 1:26

Deuteronomy 6:4

Isaiah 64:3–4

Matthew 28:19

What does Paul say in **Romans 3:4** about human attempts to "iron out" or "solve" or "make sense" of the seemingly contradictory things that God says about Himself?

When the prophet Job encountered things about God that he could not fully understand or explain, what did he wisely do? Briefly review God's speech in **Job 38–39**, and then read Job's response in **40:4–5**.

For what does David pray in **Psalm 119:18**?

Wisdom from Above

What do the following verses say about human ability to perceive and understand the mysteries of God?

Isaiah 55:8–9

1 Corinthians 2:14

James 3:14–17

Why is it vitally important for you that the mysteries of God cannot be understood or perceived on the basis of human intellect and thinking?

Who Was That Crucified Man?

What do the following verses clearly state about the man who was crucified?

Mark 15:39

John 3:16

Galatians 4:4–5

Why is the death of God's Son a greater sacrifice than the death of God the Father, if such a death were even possible (as patripassionism claims)?

Section Two

Second Article

And in Jesus Christ, His only Son, our Lord, who was conceived by the Holy Spirit, born of the Virgin Mary, suffered under Pontius Pilate, was crucified, died and was buried. He descended into hell. The third day He rose again from the dead. He ascended into heaven and sits at the right hand of God, the Father Almighty. From thence He will come to judge the living and the dead.

What does this mean?

I believe that Jesus Christ, true God, begotten of the Father from eternity, and also true man, born of the Virgin Mary, is my Lord,

who has redeemed me, a lost and condemned person, purchased and won me from all sins, from death, and from the power of the devil; not with gold or silver, but with His holy, precious blood and with His innocent suffering and death,

that I may be His own and live under Him in His kingdom and serve Him in everlasting righteousness, innocence, and blessedness,

just as He is risen from the dead, lives and reigns to all eternity.

This is most certainly true.

5

Nestorians

Lesson Focus

Wanting to keep the two natures of Christ as far separate as possible, Nestorius taught that there was absolutely no communion, or sharing of characteristics, between Jesus' divine and human natures. This teaching will tempt you to think that the Sacrament of the Altar is an empty and powerless meal.

Historical Context

Not long after Nestorius became the bishop of the Church in Constantinople in 428 AD, he ignited conflict by declaring that Mary should not be called *theotokos*, that is, "Mother of God." For Nestorius, it was impossible for God to be confined in a womb! Cyril, the Bishop of Alexandria, led a churchwide effort to get Nestorius to change his teaching. When Nestorius refused, the Council of Ephesus condemned him in 431 AD.

Nestorianism is not merely a fifth-century conflict. During the days of the Reformation, a man named Ulrich Zwingli (1484–1531) began to teach that the human body and blood of Christ could not possibly be present in the Sacrament of the Altar. Zwingli and his followers argued:

> **If Christ's body were present at the same time in heaven and on earth in the Holy Supper, it could be no real, true human body. For such majesty was said to be peculiar to God alone. [The Zwinglians] said Christ's body was not capable of it. . . . They said that nothing should be credited to the human nature in the person of Christ that is above or contrary to its natural, essential property. (Solid Declaration of the Formula of Concord, Article VIII, paragraphs 2–4)**

This helps illustrate a reason why the Nestorian heresy is so destructive. If Mary's Son, Jesus, cannot be present in the Sacrament of the Altar, then this meal offers you no help and medicine against your inherited disease of sin.

Distribute copies of Participant Page 5 if desired. Read aloud the Historical Context, above, and the Message from the Lutheran Confessions. Then pray responsively the Opening Prayer.

A Message from the Lutheran Confessions

Our doctrine, faith, and confession about the person of Christ is not divided, as it was by Nestorius. He denied the true communion of the properties of both natures in Christ (*communicatio idiomatum*). So he divided the person. (Epitome of the Formula of Concord, Article VIII, paragraph 18)

Opening Prayer

L: For to us a child is born, to us a son is given; and the government shall be upon His shoulder,

P: And His name shall be called Wonderful Counselor, Mighty God, Everlasting Father, Prince of Peace. (Isaiah 9:6)

L: For in Him the whole fullness of deity dwells bodily. (Colossians 2:9)

P: He was manifested in the flesh, vindicated by the Spirit, seen by angels, proclaimed among the nations, believed on in the world, taken up in glory. (1 Timothy 3:16)

L: Forever, O LORD, Your word is firmly fixed in the heavens.

P: Your faithfulness endures to all generations. (Psalm 119:89–90a)

And Was Made Man

Nestorius taught that Mary did not give birth to God, but that Mary's Son, Jesus, was merely adopted as the Son of God. How do the following Bible verses help you respond to such a claim?

Luke 1:35—God's angel Gabriel announced that Mary would give birth not to a mere human child, but to a human child who would be, at the same time, the Son of God. While Mary was pregnant, her relative Elizabeth also called her "the mother of my Lord" (v. 43).

Galatians 4:4–5—Notice the verb: God *sent* His Son. Contrary to the Nestorian claim, God the Father did not adopt Jesus of Nazareth as His Son, but God *sent* His Son to be born of a woman. Although Jesus was not adopted by God, He made it possible for us to "receive adoption as sons" (v. 5).

Colossians 2:9—Jesus did not merely claim to be divine or divinely adopted. "In Him the whole fullness of deity dwells in bodily form." No one can explain how it happens that humanity and divinity dwell together in Christ. This is a great and wonderful mystery, "such a grand, intimate, indescribable communion that even the angels are astonished by it. As St. Peter testifies, they have their delight and joy in looking into it [1 Peter 1:12]" (Solid Declaration of the Formula of Concord, Article VIII, paragraph 30).

According to Hebrews 2:14 and Revelation 1:17–18, why is it so important that Jesus was not merely adopted as God's Son, but that He is truly God's Son in human flesh? Hebrews 2:14 states that Jesus took our humanity into Himself, sharing our flesh and blood, so that He could destroy the inherited power of death and the devil, which had become embedded in our flesh and blood, thus enslaving us. Revelation 1:17–18 assures us that Jesus, whose divinity indicates that He is mighty enough to defeat death and hell, holds the keys of death and hell. Why should we fear these things now that our God has unlocked the door and released us from these things?

Are the divine and human natures still joined together in Jesus yet today, or did His two natures separate after His death and resurrection? See Hebrews 13:8. Hebrews 13:8 is essential for understanding the two natures of Christ. If Jesus was both God and man during His earthly life, then He still is both God and man, now and forever! Where Jesus' divine nature is now present, His human nature is likewise present. If Jesus' divine nature now fills all things (Ephesians 4:10), then His human nature likewise fills all things.

God and Man Eternally with You

God gave His Son, Jesus, the name Immanuel. *According to Matthew 1:23, what does* Immanuel *mean?* Immanuel does not mean "God once was with us" or "God will someday again be with us." *Immanuel* means "God with us."

According to Matthew 28:20 and Hebrews 13:5, for how long shall our God remain with us? Jesus, the God-man, promises that He will be with you always, "to the end of the age." *Never* will Jesus leave you or forsake you.

Return to Hebrews 13:8. According to that verse, is Jesus' divine nature or His human nature with us always? Both! Because Jesus, the God-man, is with you always, you always receive the full benefit of both His natures. You have the benefit of His humanity, which is fully acquainted with your temptations, your suffering, and your grief. You also share His divinity, which has powerfully defeated sin, death, and hell for you! This is why the early Lutherans rejoiced to say:

> **He has promised them [Christians] that not only His mere divinity would be with them (which to us poor sinners is like a consuming fire on dry stubble). But Christ promised that He—He, the man who has spoken with them, who has experienced all tribulations in His received human nature, and who can therefore have sympathy with us, as with men and His brethren—He will be with us in all our troubles also according to the nature by which He is our brother and we are flesh of His flesh. (Solid Declaration of the Formula of Concord, Article VIII, paragraph 87)**

This Is My Body

In Matthew 26:26–29, what verb does Jesus use as He describes the bread and the wine in Sacrament of the Altar? Jesus uses the verb *is*, which He states deliberately and emphatically in the Greek: "This *is* My body. . . . This *is* My blood" (vv. 26, 28, emphasis added). The verb *is* does not mean "represents" or "symbolizes" or "stands for." *Is* means "is."

In what way do 1 Corinthians 10:16 and 11:27 further help you understand the bread and the wine in the Sacrament of the Altar? When you drink of the cup and eat the bread in the Sacrament of the Altar, you participate not in a mere meal of wine and bread, but "in the blood of Christ" and "in the body of Christ" (1 Corinthians 10:16). How would it be possible to participate in the blood and body of Jesus if He is not even present there in the cup and in the bread?

Paul also warns that those who eat and drink the Sacrament unworthily commit sin. They are not held guilty of profaning bread and wine, but "guilty concerning the body and blood of the Lord" (1 Corinthians 11:27). How is it possible to profane a body and blood that are not present?

"Nothing should be credited to the human nature in the person of Christ that is above or contrary to its natural, essential property." In what way does this Zwinglian/Nestorian claim make it impossible to take the Bible verses above at face value? If you presuppose that it is impossible for Jesus' humanity to share any of the characteristics of His divinity, then you will blind yourself to what the Scriptures teach you about Holy Communion. If Jesus' humanity cannot be present everywhere, as His divinity is, then His humanity cannot be present in the Sacrament of the Altar. People who follow the Zwinglian/Nestorian line of thinking simply cannot agree that *is* means "is" in Matthew 26:26–28. This is why many Lutherans find it frustrating to discuss the Sacrament of the Altar with non-Lutherans.

What benefits might you prevent yourself from receiving when you cannot believe what Jesus says about the Sacrament of the Altar? If the bread and wine are not Jesus' body and blood, then the bread and wine are also not able to deliver the forgiveness of sins to you. Because the bread and wine cannot give you forgiveness of sins, they also cannot give you strength to resist the temptations of the world, the devil, and your own inherited sin. Nor can mere bread and wine give you any comfort against your fear of death.

This is, in part, the present-day tragedy of Nestorian thinking: the separation of Christ's two natures renders the Sacrament of the Altar powerless to help you in your daily need.

Closing Prayer

Dearest Jesus, You are both Mary's Son and our God! By the power of Your Word and Spirit, enable us to trust and believe that where Your divinity is, there Your humanity is also, most especially so that we may never doubt or devalue the gifts that You give to us in Your Holy Sacrament. Amen.

5

Nestorians

A Message from the Lutheran Confessions

Our doctrine, faith, and confession about the person of Christ is not divided, as it was by Nestorius. He denied the true communion of the properties of both natures in Christ (*communicatio idiomatum*). So he divided the person. (Epitome of the Formula of Concord, Article VIII, paragraph 18)

Opening Prayer

L: For to us a child is born, to us a son is given; and the government shall be upon His shoulder,

P: And His name shall be called Wonderful Counselor, Mighty God, Everlasting Father, Prince of Peace. (Isaiah 9:6)

L: For in Him the whole fullness of deity dwells bodily. (Colossians 2:9)

P: He was manifested in the flesh, vindicated by the Spirit, seen by angels, proclaimed among the nations, believed on in the world, taken up in glory. (1 Timothy 3:16)

L: Forever, O Lord, Your word is firmly fixed in the heavens.

P: Your faithfulness endures to all generations. (Psalm 119:89–90a)

And Was Made Man

Nestorius taught that Mary did not give birth to God, but that Mary's Son, Jesus, was merely adopted as the Son of God. How do the following Bible verses help you respond to such a claim?

Luke 1:35

Galatians 4:4–5

Colossians 2:9

According to **Hebrews 2:14** and **Revelation 1:17–18**, why is it so important that Jesus was not merely adopted as God's Son, but that Jesus is truly God's Son in human flesh?

Are the divine and human natures still joined together in Jesus yet today, or did His two natures separate after His death and resurrection? See **Hebrews 13:8**.

God and Man Eternally with You

God gave His Son, Jesus, the name *Immanuel*. According to **Matthew 1:23**, what does *Immanuel* mean?

According to **Matthew 28:20** and **Hebrews 13:5**, for how long shall our God remain with us?

Return to **Hebrews 13:8**. According to that verse, is Jesus' divine nature or His human nature with us always?

This Is My Body

In **Matthew 26:26–29**, what verb does Jesus use as He describes the bread and the wine in the Sacrament of the Altar?

In what way do **1 Corinthians 10:16** and **11:27** further help you understand the bread and the wine in the Sacrament of the Altar?

"Nothing should be credited to the human nature in the person of Christ that is above or contrary to its natural, essential property." In what way does this Zwinglian/Nestorian claim make it impossible to take the Bible verses above at face value?

What benefits might you prevent yourself from receiving when you cannot believe what Jesus says about the Sacrament of the Altar?

6

Lesson Focus

Eutyches taught that the divine and human natures of Christ mixed together into a single, new, hybrid nature. This teaching will tempt you to think that your Lord Jesus Christ did not fully experience and share every temptation and hardship that you suffer, since He had a superhuman advantage over you.

Historical Context

As a church leader in Constantinople, Eutyches so deeply opposed Nestorius (Lesson 5) that he went to the other extreme. Eutyches mixed Christ's two natures together into one new nature. This idea of mixing the natures is called Monophysitism (*mono* = Greek for "one"; *physis* = Greek for "nature").

It might come as no surprise that the Zwinglians (Lesson 5) accused Martin Luther and the early Lutheran reformers of Eutychianism. This accusation was made because the Lutherans believed there is such a close relationship between Christ's humanity and divinity that the characteristics of one nature are shared with, or communicated to, the other nature. (For example, it is accurate to say, "Our God died on the cross," even though death is impossible for someone who is eternal. Christ's human capability of death was communicated to His divine nature.) However, the communion of Christ's two natures does *not* mean the natures mixed together into one new nature, as Eutyches claimed! This is why the Lutherans confessed in their Book of Concord, "For in no way is conversion, confusion, or equalization of the natures in Christ or of their essential properties to be made or allowed" (Solid Declaration of the Formula of Concord, Article VIII, paragraph 62).

Does this amount to splitting hairs? Absolutely not! If the two natures of Christ are mixed, then you have a *super*human Savior, rather than a human Savior. Thus it would have been easier for Jesus to resist temptation than it is for you. This is simply not the case.

Distribute copies of Participant Page 6 if desired. Read aloud the Historical Context, above, and the Message from the Lutheran Confessions. Then pray responsively the Opening Prayer.

A Message from the Lutheran Confessions

The natures [of Christ], together with their properties, are not mixed with each other into one essence (as Eutyches erred). The human nature in the person of Christ is not denied or annihilated. Nor is either nature changed into the other. Christ is and remains to all eternity God and man in one undivided person. (Epitome of the Formula of Concord, Article VIII, paragraph 18)

Opening Prayer

L: Since therefore the children share in flesh and blood, He Himself likewise partook of the same things,

P: **That through death He might destroy the one who has the power of death, that is, the devil.** (Hebrews 2:14)

L: For there is one God, and there is one mediator between God and men,

P: **The man Christ Jesus.** (1 Timothy 2:5)

L: Forever, O LORD, Your word is firmly fixed in the heavens.

P: **Your faithfulness endures to all generations.** (Psalm 119:89–90a)

Able to Sympathize with Our Weakness

According to Hebrews 4:15, why is it vitally important for you that Jesus' two natures did not mix together into a single, new nature? If Jesus' two natures had become mixed, He could not have fully sympathized with our weakness or have been tempted in every way that we are. Here is an analogy: The high school bully who frightens and terrorizes a child who is small for his or her age might not seem so scary to someone who is as large as the bully. In a similar way, if Jesus' two natures were mixed together into a new, superhuman nature, He would not be like the small child who is frightened by the bully. Thus, Jesus would not feel the same weight of temptation and weakness that we ourselves feel.

According to the same verse, what is the single way in which Jesus is different from you? Does this difference mean Jesus was not actually, fully human?
Jesus is like us in every respect, "yet without sin" (Hebrews 4:15). However, Jesus' sinless perfection does not mean that He is not fully human. The old saying "To err is human" is wrong. The horrible disease of sin is a foreign intrusion that became *embedded* in our humanity. Sin is not an original characteristic or attribute of humanity. After all, God created humanity, but God does not create sin! Thus, Jesus participated fully and completely in every aspect of our humanity, "yet without sin."

What do the following Bible verses say about Jesus' participation in your weaknesses and hardships?

Matthew 4:2—"He was hungry." Jesus experienced bodily hunger and its painful effects, just as anyone who misses several meals would feel such things.

John 11:33–38—"Jesus wept" (v. 35). While it is certainly possible that Jesus wept on account of His deep love and compassion for Lazarus, Mary, and Martha, perhaps our Lord's tears were also motivated by the scene He saw playing out before His eyes. It is almost as if the story of Lazarus were an Easter pageant, so to speak: Jews were coming out from Jerusalem, as would later happen at Jesus' own crucifixion. Lazarus's tomb was a cave with a stone at the entrance, just like the cave in which our Lord was to be laid. Is it possible that Jesus, fully sinless and without fear, wept at the weakness and human frailty of His own impending death?

Mark 14:35–36—"Remove this cup from Me" (v. 36). No sane human relishes the thought of suffering and pain. Jesus, fully human like you and me, prays that God His Father might perhaps find another way for the redemption of the world to be accomplished.

What help do the following verses give you for understanding the role Jesus' divinity played in His suffering?

Matthew 26:52–53—Jesus is God's Son, and God loves Him so much that He would send legions of angels to His Son's defense. Yet Jesus refused to invoke His divinity in order to save Himself. Rather, Jesus' divinity remained quiet within Him, not defending Him from any attack.

Philippians 2:5–8—Jesus "made Himself nothing" (v. 7). This does not mean that Jesus threw away His divinity, but that the power and influence of His divinity amounted to nothing while He suffered.

Colossians 1:22—Jesus reconciled you to God, not by the power of His divine nature, but "in His body of flesh by His death."

A Trusty Shield and Strong Defense

Read Matthew 4:1–11. What weapon did Jesus use against the temptations of the devil? For each of Jesus' temptations, He guarded Himself against falling into sin by means of the written Word of God. This is good news for you, because it means that you have the very same weaponry at your defense when you likewise are tempted! Jesus did not exercise any divine ability to resist temptation, because you have no divine abilities of your own. Jesus suffered the same temptations that you suffer, and He used the same weapon of defense that God has likewise placed into your hands: "It is written. . . . It is written. . . . It is written. . . ."

Compare Matthew 4:1–11 and Mark 1:9–13. What is noticeably absent in Mark's version of Jesus' temptation? According to the immediate context, what power and strength did Jesus rely upon while tempted? Jesus' use of the Scriptures as a defense against temptation is noticeably absent in Mark's Gospel. It is not that Mark did not want you to know how Jesus used the Scriptures. Rather, Mark focuses your attention on another powerful weapon that you and Jesus share. What happened immediately before Jesus' temptation? He was baptized! By not spelling out all the Bible verses that Jesus used to defend Himself against the devil, Mark is showing you how Baptism provides you with a similarly powerful defense.

In what way do these two passages, above, deliver great comfort and strength to you for when you likewise suffer temptations? Jesus endures in the same manner that you also can endure. Jesus has no advantage over you in suffering and temptation. Jesus makes certain aspects of His divinity lie dormant, and He experiences all that you experience, using the same tools of defense that you also have been given—the Scriptures and your Baptism.

What additional help does Isaiah 53:2–3 provide? Isaiah emphasizes Jesus' humanity by calling Him "a man of sorrows" and someone who is "acquainted with grief" (v. 3). Jesus could not even rely on His good looks as a way of getting through life! "He had no form or majesty that we should look at Him, and no beauty that we should desire Him" (v. 2). All Jesus had is what you have: the powerful, life-giving Word of God.

Closing Prayer

Dearest Jesus, Your humanness is mine and mine is Yours in every way, except for my sin. By the power of Your Word and Spirit, guard and protect me from all temptation by means of the same powerful gifts that You Yourself used in self-defense during the days of Your weakness. Amen.

6

A Message from the Lutheran Confessions

The natures [of Christ], together with their properties, are not mixed with each other into one essence (as Eutyches erred). The human nature in the person of Christ is not denied or annihilated. Nor is either nature changed into the other. Christ is and remains to all eternity God and man in one undivided person. (Epitome of the Formula of Concord, Article VIII, paragraph 18)

Opening Prayer

L: Since therefore the children share in flesh and blood, He Himself likewise partook of the same things,

P: That through death He might destroy the one who has the power of death, that is, the devil. (Hebrews 2:14)

L: For there is one God, and there is one mediator between God and men,

P: The man Christ Jesus. (1 Timothy 2:5)

L: Forever, O LORD, Your word is firmly fixed in the heavens.

P: Your faithfulness endures to all generations. (Psalm 119:89–90a)

Able to Sympathize with our Weakness

According to **Hebrews 4:15**, why is it vitally important for you that Jesus' two natures did *not* mix together into a single, new nature?

According to the same verse, what is the single way in which Jesus is different from you? Does this difference mean Jesus was not actually, fully human?

What do the following Bible verses say about Jesus' participation in your weaknesses and hardships?

Matthew 4:2

John 11:33–38

Mark 14:35–36

What help do the following verses give you for understanding the role Jesus' divinity played in His suffering?

Matthew 26:52–53

Philippians 2:5–8

Colossians 1:22

A Trusty Shield and Strong Defense

Read **Matthew 4:1–11**. What weapon did Jesus use against the temptations of the devil?

Compare **Matthew 4:1–11** and **Mark 1:9–13**. What is noticeably absent in Mark's version of Jesus' temptation? According to the immediate context, what power and strength did Jesus rely upon while tempted?

In what way do these two passages, above, deliver great comfort and strength to you for when you likewise suffer temptations?

What additional help does **Isaiah 53:2–3** provide?

7

Docetists

Lesson Focus

The varieties of Docetism share a common theme: Christ did not actually suffer torment and death in a human body. Among other things, this teaching will tempt you to think that your God will abandon you when times get tough.

Historical Context

Although this heresy predates Nestorianism (Lesson 5), Docetism similarly denies the connection between the two natures of Christ. Rooted in Gnosticism (Lesson 9), various Docetic teachers claimed a drastic disconnect between Christ's humanity and divinity, based on the idea that God is incapable of suffering:

Cerinthus (ca. 100 AD) taught that Christ descended upon Jesus in the form of a dove at His Baptism, and then left Jesus immediately prior to the crucifixion.

Saturninus (second century AD) taught that our Savior, unborn and bodiless, was only an apparition that looked like a man.

Apollinaris of Laodicea (fourth century AD) taught that Jesus Christ did not have a human soul. Rather, the Word (Logos) took the place of Jesus' human soul.

Bishops and pastors in the Early Church quickly realized the disastrous consequence of Docetism: if Christ escaped suffering and death, then there is no salvation! Docetism was opposed by the good and faithful slogan "What Christ has not assumed, He has not redeemed [or healed]." This slogan meant that if Christ did not have a human body, He did not redeem your human body; if He did not have a human spirit, He did not redeem your spirit, and so forth. Opposition to Docetism led to the Athanasian Creed, a confession of faith still used today by many Christians, including Lutherans: "He [Jesus Christ] is God, begotten from the substance of the Father before all ages; and He is man, born from the substance of His mother in this age: perfect God and perfect man, composed of a rational soul and human flesh" (*LSB*, page 320).

Distribute copies of Participant Page 7 if desired. Read aloud the Historical Context, above, and the Message from Martin Luther. Then pray responsively the Opening Prayer.

A Message from Martin Luther

In one Person He [Jesus Christ] is both true God together with the Father and true man born of the Virgin. . . . This is the doctrine which the devil has always seized on, which is still assailed and will suffer from manifold heresies until the Day of Judgment. For some have made the blasphemous statement that Christ was only a make-believe or a phantom and not a true man. (Luther's Works, American Edition, Volume 24, pages 90–91)

Opening Prayer

L: [Jesus] said to Thomas, "Put your finger here, and see My hands;

P: And put out your hand, and place it in My side.

L: Do not disbelieve, but believe."

P: Thomas answered Him, "My Lord and my God!" (John 20:27–28)

L: Forever, O LORD, Your word is firmly fixed in the heavens.

P: Your faithfulness endures to all generations. (Psalm 119:89–90a)

The Suffering God

How do the following verses support the idea that God cannot suffer?

Malachi 3:6—"I the LORD do not change."

James 1:17—Every good gift comes from "the Father of lights with whom there is no variation or shadow due to change."

Psalm 102:26–27—Everything changes, except God: "You are the same" (v. 27).

On the surface, these verses all emphasize that there is no change in God. Since suffering presupposes change, these verses also lead to the good conclusion that God cannot suffer: if God cannot change, He therefore cannot suffer, since the end product of suffering would be a crushed, damaged, altered version of the original.

Discuss why it is so important for you to know and to believe that God does not change. No one wants a God who changes like the shadows or the shifting wind! How could you ever know where you stood with such a God, or whether He will be happy with you in one moment and angry with you the next? God's changelessness is a gift for you, so that you may trust and rely upon Him and upon His promises.

Some people might argue that God the Son truly underwent a change when He was conceived by the Holy Spirit in Mary's womb. What help do the following Bible verses provide in answering such an argument?

John 1:14—When John states "the Word . . . dwelt among us," he uses the word for "tabernacled" or "tented." God the Son did not change when He became human, but rather, He took human flesh upon Himself, somewhat like putting on clothing. You could say that Jesus is God the Son who clothed Himself in human flesh.

Romans 8:3—God sent His Son "in the likeness of sinful flesh." That is, Jesus took the very form and nature of those who suffer sin in their flesh, "yet without sin" (Hebrews 4:15).

Philippians 2:7 and Colossians 2:9—Jesus took the form—in Greek, the *morphe*—of a servant in Philippians 2:7. This was not a mere phantom or apparition, but a "bodily" form (Colossians 2:9).

These verses express the great, nearly indescribable mystery of the incarnation, in which God the Son became man by drawing humanity into Himself and by clothing Himself with our human bodies and nature.

In what way do 1 John 1:2–4 and 2:2 describe Jesus as the God who suffers? John calls Jesus "the propitiation"—that is, the atoning sacrifice—for our sins (1 John 2:2). Yet, just before this statement, John called Jesus "the eternal life" and the Son of God (1:2–4).

How, then, is it possible that the unchangeable God might experience suffering?

Galatians 4:4–5—God the Son did not change, but reduced Himself to be born of a woman and under the Law. That is to say, God the Son miraculously joined Himself to the humanity Mary gave to Him when He was conceived.

Hebrews 2:14—God the Son shared in our weakness and our death so that He could overcome the one who kept us pinned in weakness and death, that is, the devil.

In both cases, Jesus' divinity draws so inseparably close to His humanity that the two natures can communicate, or share, attributes and characteristics. One ancient (somewhat limited) analogy is that of a piece of iron heated to red hot in the fire. The iron does not change, but the attributes of the fire get shared with the iron. In the same way, God the Son drew humanity into Himself so that His divinity shares characteristics with His humanity, and vice versa. For this reason, we can faithfully say such things as "My God died on the cross" and "Jesus' human body and blood are miraculously present in the Sacrament of the Altar." This is why it is also written, "He Himself bore our sins *in His body* on the tree, that we might die to sin and live to righteousness" (1 Peter 2:24, emphasis added).

My Lord and My God

In what way does John 20:24–29 provide you with a strong argument against the heresy of Docetism? Thomas shows you that Jesus was not merely a phantom, but that His is a true human body. Thomas demanded that he place his hands into the wounds that pierced his Lord, and the Lord allowed him to do so! If Jesus were a phantom, Thomas would have had nothing to touch.

I Will Be with You

If God could not be with Jesus in His suffering, as the Docetists claimed, then He cannot be with you in your suffering, either. In what way do the following verses show how Jesus is unafraid to be near to those who suffer?

Mark 1:41; 7:32–33; and Luke 7:11–14—These verses each show how Jesus placed His physical hands upon those who were leprous and deaf and even dead.

Luke 15:1–2—Jesus happily welcomes the lowest sinners and those who have the worst reputations.

These are precious verses for sinful people! Not only do these verses support the truth that Jesus possessed a human body, but they also show you how Jesus does not want to stay distant from you, even when you suffer or fall into sin. Cerinthus taught that Christ "jumped ship," so to speak, in order to avoid the suffering of the cross. But the Jesus Christ spoken about in the Bible endures with you in suffering, holding you in His hands, undeterred by your sin!

More than being with you in suffering, what do the following verses say about your Lord's participation in your suffering?

Isaiah 53:4–5—Jesus is not merely with you in suffering hardship, but He suffered all things before you and for your sake. Your God is not unfamiliar with your experiences, but rather, "He was wounded for our transgressions; He was crushed for our iniquities" (v. 5).

Psalm 23—The Lord is your gentle shepherd who not only walks with you "through the valley of the shadow of death" (v. 4), but who also actively fights and protects you from the enemy by means of His rod and staff, which He knows well how to use.

What connection does Jesus draw between Psalm 23 and Himself in John 10:11? Jesus wants you to know that He personally is your shepherd who leads you in paths of righteousness. That is why He repeatedly says in John 10, "I am the good shepherd."

Closing Prayer

You are my Lord and my God, Jesus, whose suffering for my salvation was displayed in the wounds in Your human hands and human chest. By the power of Your Word and Spirit, strengthen my faith always to believe that You remain eternally with me, no matter what my human body might suffer or endure. Amen.

7

Docetists

A Message from Martin Luther

In one Person He [Jesus Christ] is both true God together with the Father and true man born of the Virgin. . . . This is the doctrine which the devil has always seized on, which is still assailed and will suffer from manifold heresies until the Day of Judgment. For some have made the blasphemous statement that Christ was only a make-believe or a phantom and not a true man. (Luther's Works, American Edition, Volume 24, pages 90–91)

Opening Prayer

L: [Jesus] said to Thomas, "Put your finger here, and see My hands;

P: And put out your hand, and place it in My side.

L: Do not disbelieve, but believe."

P: Thomas answered Him, "My Lord and my God!" (John 20:27–28)

L: Forever, O Lord, Your word is firmly fixed in the heavens.

P: Your faithfulness endures to all generations. (Psalm 119:89–90a)

The Suffering God

How do the following verses support the idea that God cannot suffer?
Malachi 3:6

James 1:17

Psalm 102:26–27

Discuss why it is so important for you to know and to believe that God does not change.

Some people might argue that God the Son underwent a change when He was conceived by the Holy Spirit in Mary's womb. What help do the following Bible verses provide in answering such an argument?
John 1:14

Romans 8:3

Philippians 2:7 and **Colossians 2:9**

In what way do **1 John 1:2–4** and **2:2** describe Jesus as the God who suffers?

How, then, is it possible that the unchangeable God might experience suffering?

Galatians 4:4–5

Hebrews 2:14

1 Peter 2:24

My Lord and My God

In what way does **John 20:24–29** provide you with a strong argument against the heresy of Docetism?

I Will Be with You

If God could not be with Jesus in His suffering, as the Docetists claimed, then He cannot be with you in your suffering either. In what way do the following verses show how Jesus is unafraid to be near to those who suffer?

Mark 1:41; 7:32–33; and **Luke 7:11–14**

Luke 15:1–2

More than being with you in suffering, what do the following verses say about your Lord's participation in your suffering?

Isaiah 53:4–5

Psalm 23

What connection does Jesus draw between **Psalm 23** and Himself in **John 10:11**?

8

Montanists

Lesson Focus

Montanism is one of the earliest expressions of the false teaching that Christ will establish a thousand-year reign on earth. This teaching tempts you to think that you can do something to hasten Christ's coming, or that you will be given a new opportunity for repentance if you should be "left behind."

Historical Context

Living in the latter part of the second century AD, Montanus began with good intentions. The earliest Christians had kept a high expectation for Christ's immediate, final return. When Christ did not return as quickly as they hoped, many Christians stopped living a strictly moral life and allowed their attention to be diverted to worldly things. Wanting to return the Church's attention to high expectation for Christ's return, Montanus proclaimed himself to be the Paraclete (or "Helper") whom Christ had promised to send (John 15:26).

Working with two prophetesses, Priscilla and Maximilla, Montanus claimed to have received a special message directly from God, apart from the Scriptures (Gnostics, Lesson 9). Montanus began teaching that Christ was indeed coming back: He would arrive in the city of Pepuza in Phrygia, and would there establish a one-thousand-year reign. (This teaching is called "millennialism" or "chiliasm.") Montanus and his followers even gathered in Pepuza, standing on a hillside, staring at the sky, waiting for the big event that never occurred.

Since Montanus, many Christians have found it appealing to think that Christ will establish a millennial reign here on earth. Not only is this teaching untrue, but it also moves your attention off Christ and onto yourself: you will either spur yourself into many "preparations" for Christ's arrival, as Montanus hoped, or you will put off your repentance for another day.

Distribute copies of Participant Page 8 if desired. Read aloud the Historical Context, above, and the Message from Martin Luther. Then pray responsively the Opening Prayer.

A Message from Martin Luther

The Anabaptists and similar erring spirits dream that before the Last Day all the enemies of the church will be physically exterminated and a church assembled which shall consist of pious Christians only; they will govern in peace, without any opposition or attack. But this text [Psalm 110:1] clearly and powerfully says that there are to be enemies continuously as long as this Christ reigns on earth. And certain it is, too, that death will not be abolished until the Last Day, when all His enemies will be exterminated with one blow. (Luther's Works, American Edition, Volume 13, pages 263–64)

Opening Prayer

L: The LORD says to my Lord: "Sit at My right hand, until I make Your enemies Your footstool."
(Psalm 110:1)

P: **Then comes the end, when [Jesus] delivers the kingdom to God the Father after destroying every rule and every authority and power.**

L: For He must reign until He has put all His enemies under His feet.

P: **The last enemy to be destroyed is death.**
(1 Corinthians 15:24–26)

L: Forever, O LORD, Your word is firmly fixed in the heavens.

P: **Your faithfulness endures to all generations.**
(Psalm 119:89–90a)

The Kingdom of Christ

Revelation 20:1–7 is a main "proof" for teaching millennialism. Discuss how this passage might indeed lead someone to believe that Christ will reign on earth for a literal one-thousand-year period. The phrase "a thousand years" is repeated several times in this passage. Read quickly, it certainly could seem as though this phrase refers to the literal, thousand-year, earthly reign of Christ taught by millennialists ancient and modern.

What elements of Revelation 20:1–7 are clearly symbolic? How do these many symbols shape the way you think about the one thousand years? While not every part of this passage is easily explained, this passage is stuffed with symbolism! Here are some examples:

1. It is not a literal chain, made of iron or steel, that binds Satan, who is a spirit

being. The chain is a symbol of Christ's miraculous strength, by which Satan's influence has now been limited and restricted.

2. The bottomless pit and its cover are likewise symbols of hell, which is not a defined, literal location beneath the earth.

3. The angel represents Christ, whose death and resurrection finally defeated Satan.

With these symbols in Revelation 20:1–7, it is good to think that the thousand years is likewise a symbol, and not a literal period of time. Considering also the way some Jewish writing employed symbolic meanings to numbers, many theologians and Bible scholars suggest that one thousand symbolizes the completion of the New Testament Era, that is, the time between Christ's ascension and His return. These scholars say that ten is the symbolic number for completeness, and the cube of ten—one thousand—indicates "supercompleteness" or total completeness.

In what way do Psalm 90:4 and 2 Peter 3:8 support the idea that one thousand years is symbolic? Both verses compare one day to a thousand years, or "a really long time." The point is not the literal passage of a thousand-year era, but that God is not limited by time in any way. If God cannot be limited by time, why would we want to think He has locked Himself into a thousand-year earthly reign before the end of time?

No One Knows

People who teach a millennial reign of Christ will often go further and claim to know the date when it will happen. What does Jesus say about this in Matthew 24:36, 42? Jesus assures you, "Concerning that day and hour no one knows, not even the angels of heaven, nor the Son, but the Father only. . . . *You* do not know on what day your Lord is coming" (emphasis added). Not even Jesus, within the human limitations of His earthly flesh, could know what day He would return. Whenever you hear someone claim to know the day, you can conclude that the person is a liar and intends nothing good for you.

Discuss why it is a blessing and benefit for you not to know the date or the hour of Christ's return. Suppose everyone in your class at school was given the same major assignment, due two months from today. Some of your classmates would get to work immediately and turn in their assignment as soon as possible, hoping to impress the teacher. Others would wait until the absolute last minute, then scramble to get everything done. Either way, both groups of people are focused on themselves. The "early birds" want to earn special favor or recognition, while the procrastinators feel like they have better things to do.

Something similar would happen if we knew the date and hour of our Lord's return: we would quickly want to focus on ourselves. Some Christians would hurry to do as many good things as they could, wanting to make themselves look as good as possible in the eyes of their returning Lord. (Many television preachers encourage such actions.) Other Christians would wait until the last minute, wanting to ignore God and His Word for as long as possible.

By not telling us when He will return, Jesus calls upon us simply to watch and be ready continually. This happens through careful attention to His Word and trust in His promises, and by not focusing on our own efforts!

What do the following verses say about the signs that will accompany Christ's return? As you study these verses, discuss: for how long have these signs been taking place?

Matthew 24:6–14—Wars and rumors of wars will increase as time passes; famines and earthquakes will occur; Christians will be betrayed; lawlessness will increase; faith will grow cold. These things have been taking place ever since Jesus ascended into heaven!

Luke 21:25–28—The phrase "nations in perplexity because of the roaring of the sea and the waves" sounds like the description of a tsunami or a hurricane. Storms such as these are as ancient as they are modern.

Joel 2:30–31 (compare Acts 2:14–21)—Peter says that Joel's foreboding prophecy about the sun being darkened and the moon looking like blood already found its fulfillment by the time of the first Christian Pentecost. Matthew also points out that when Jesus was crucified, "from the sixth hour there was darkness over all the land until the ninth hour" (Matthew 27:45).

The point here is simple: many false preachers point to the signs of the end times and use them to whip up millennial expectations. Such signs have been given to us as serious reminders that the end is coming—not so that we can help establish an earthly reign of Christ, but so that we will patiently watch and wait, because our "redemption is drawing near" (Luke 21:28).

Thy Kingdom Come

What do the following verses say about the return of Christ?

Matthew 24:27—Jesus' return will be sudden and unexpected, like a strike of lightning on a sunny day, and it will be evident to every person on earth at the same time.

1 Thessalonians 4:13–17—When Jesus returns, He will gather everyone immediately to Himself. The dead in Christ will rise first, and we who are still alive will rise with them into the air.

Matthew 25:31–46—When Christ returns, He will immediately judge all things.

2 Peter 3:10–13—There will be no thousand-year reign on earth, but the present earth and heavens will be destroyed.

What clear answer to millennialism does Jesus speak in John 18:36? Jesus says, "My kingdom is not of this world." Contrary to the claims of millennialists, Jesus does not wish to establish an earthly kingdom. If He did wish to do so, "My servants would have been fighting, that I might not be delivered over to the Jews. But My kingdom is not from the world."

Closing Prayer

"Amen. Come, Lord Jesus!" (Revelation 22:20). By the power of Your Word and Spirit, do not allow us to be overwhelmed or frightened by false teaching, but give us true repentance and faith, that each day, we may sincerely look forward to Your triumphant return. Amen.

8

A Message from Martin Luther

The Anabaptists and similar erring spirits dream that before the Last Day all the enemies of the church will be physically exterminated and a church assembled which shall consist of pious Christians only; they will govern in peace, without any opposition or attack. But this text [Psalm 110:1] clearly and powerfully says that there are to be enemies continuously as long as this Christ reigns on earth. And certain it is, too, that death will not be abolished until the Last Day, when all His enemies will be exterminated with one blow. (Luther's Works, American Edition, Volume 13, pages 263–64)

Opening Prayer

L: The LORD says to my Lord: "Sit at My right hand, until I make Your enemies Your footstool." (Psalm 110:1)

P: **Then comes the end, when [Jesus] delivers the kingdom to God the Father after destroying every rule and every authority and power.**

L: For He must reign until He has put all His enemies under His feet.

P: **The last enemy to be destroyed is death.** (1 Corinthians 15:24–26)

L: Forever, O LORD, Your word is firmly fixed in the heavens.

P: **Your faithfulness endures to all generations.** (Psalm 119:89–90a)

The Kingdom of Christ

Revelation 20:1–7 is a main "proof" for teaching millennialism. Discuss how this passage might indeed lead someone to believe that Christ will reign on earth for a literal one-thousand-year period.

What elements of **Revelation 20:1–7** are clearly symbolic? How do these many symbols shape the way you think about the one thousand years?

In what way do **Psalm 90:4** and **2 Peter 3:8** support the idea that one thousand years is symbolic?

No One Knows

People who teach a millennial reign of Christ will often go further and claim to know the date when it will happen. What does Jesus say about this in **Matthew 24:36, 42**?

Discuss why it is a blessing and benefit for you not to know the date or the hour of Christ's return.

What do the following verses say about the signs that will accompany Christ's return? As you study these verses, discuss: for how long have these signs been taking place?

Matthew 24:6–14

Luke 21:25–28

Joel 2:30–31 (compare **Acts 2:14–21**)

Thy Kingdom Come

What do the following verses say about the return of Christ?

Matthew 24:27

1 Thessalonians 4:13–17

Matthew 25:31–46

2 Peter 3:10–13

What clear answer to millennialism does Jesus speak in **John 18:36**?

Section Three

Third Article

**I believe in the Holy Spirit,
the holy Christian church,
the communion of saints,
the forgiveness of sins, the
resurrection of the body, and
the life everlasting. Amen.**

What does this mean?

I believe that I cannot by my own reason or
strength believe in Jesus Christ, my Lord, or
come to Him; but the Holy Spirit has called me
by the Gospel, enlightened me with His gifts,
sanctified and kept me in the true faith.

In the same way He calls, gathers, enlightens,
and sanctifies the whole Christian church on
earth, and keeps it with Jesus Christ in the one
true faith.

In this Christian church He daily and richly
forgives all my sins and the sins of all believers.

On the Last Day He will raise me and all the
dead, and give eternal life to me and all believers
in Christ.

This is most certainly true.

9

Gnostics

Lesson Focus

The varieties of Gnosticism share a common theme: God will speak to you apart from, and independent of, His written Word, the Holy Scriptures. This teaching will tempt you to believe that each "voice" you hear in your head or your heart—even those that utter your own desires—might be the "voice of God."

Historical Context

Predating the New Testament, Gnosticism became a challenge to the Christian Church almost as soon as Jesus ascended into heaven. By the second and third centuries AD, Gnosticism was a massive phenomenon, encompassing many teachers, including Simon Magus (Acts 8:9–24), Cerinthus (Lesson 7), and Montanus (Lesson 8). Various Gnostics incorporated Greek dualism (Lesson 3), cult teachings, secret names, clandestine gatherings, magical phrases, and other seemingly religious elements into their teachings. A common thread to all Gnosticism is a claim to possess secretly revealed, or personally revealed, knowledge of God—God speaking to you apart from His Word, the Scriptures, by whispering into your heart, for example. The Greek word *gnosis* means "knowledge." In Gnosticism, *gnosis* has to do with special knowledge revealed to certain people of greater spirituality or faith, which other people with lesser spirituality have not yet received. Among others, modern Pentecostals are a main example of those who carry forward the Gnostic tradition still today.

Gnosticism became a problem during the Lutheran Reformation when some reformers wanted to go further than simply removing the abuses of the Roman Church. Leading what is today called the "Radical Reformation," such leaders as Andreas Carlstadt taught people that true spirituality goes above and beyond the Word and the Sacraments. Carlstadt's teachings, in particular, led Luther and his fellow Christians to confess:

> **We must constantly maintain this point: God does not want to deal with us in any other way than through the spoken Word and the Sacraments. Whatever is praised as from the Spirit—without the Word and Sacraments—is the devil himself. (Smalcald Articles, Part III, Article VIII, paragraph 10)**

Distribute copies of Participant Page 9 if desired. Read aloud the Historical Context, above, and the Message from Martin Luther. Then pray responsively the Opening Prayer.

A Message from Martin Luther

Different spirits come along . . . and claim that they are the ones who have the Spirit. Their one boast is of nothing but the Spirit. And they bring some fine and alluring arguments and attractive words, as the Anabaptists and their ilk do today, and in years past the Montanists and many others did. Our whole quarrel with all these factions revolves about their claim that they have the Holy Spirit and that therefore they should be believed. (Luther's Works, American Edition, Volume 24, pages 176–77)

Opening Prayer

L: Long ago, at many times and in many ways, God spoke to our fathers by the prophets,

P: But in these last days He has spoken to us by His Son. (Hebrews 1:1–2a)

L: Do not add to His words,

P: Lest He rebuke you and you be found a liar. (Proverbs 30:6)

L: Forever, O Lord, Your word is firmly fixed in the heavens.

P: Your faithfulness endures to all generations. (Psalm 119:89–90a)

All Is Said That Shall Be Said

What does Hebrews 1:1–2 say about the way God desires to speak to us, especially now that Jesus was born, suffered, died, and rose again? An important part of Hebrews 1:1–2 is the phrase "has spoken" in "He has spoken to us by His Son." The Greek word for "has spoken" is an aorist participle, which emphasizes an action that is now fully complete. The idea here is, "God has finally and completely spoken to us through Jesus, and now He has nothing more He wishes to say." Jesus, in other words, is the sum total of what God the Father wishes to say to us. No new revelations (such as the Gnostics sought) are needed—in fact, such revelations are contrary to the faith—because Jesus Himself is God's full and complete message to us.

Many theologians and Bible scholars note that some of the apostle John's writings were directed against early Gnostics. What warning does John speak in Revelation 22:18–19? Do not add or subtract from this book, that is, the collection of various writings that comprise the Bible! John even speaks a curse upon those who would claim to add prophecies or revelations to the completed prophecy of the New Testament: "God will add to him the plagues described in this book" (v. 18). That is to say, those who add to what God has said, by claiming secret revelations from God, will suffer every plague ever suffered by anyone in the Old or New Testament (including the plagues of the exodus and the plagues described in Revelation and every plague in between).

According to Deuteronomy 4:2; 12:32; and Proverbs 30:6, is John's warning in Revelation 22:18–19 a new idea? From the earliest days of the exodus, God warned His people not to add to the Word of God. Solomon, the wisest man who ever lived, also thought it wise not to add to God's Words.

The Lutheran reformers said, "God does not want to deal with us in any other way than through the spoken Word and the Sacraments" (Smalcald Articles, Part III, Article VIII, paragraph 10). Why is it so absolutely essential for you that God confine Himself to speaking only through His Word and Sacraments? If God speaks inwardly into your heart and mind, as many Pentecostals claim, how can you distinguish between His will and your own personal wants or desires? The only way to be certain that you are hearing the voice of God is to direct your attention to His Word and His Sacraments. These things faithfully speak His Word to you, no matter what the condition of your emotions or your mental state.

What does Peter emphasize in the last portion of 2 Peter 1:16–19? After speaking about how he and his fellow apostles heard "the voice [that] was borne to Him [Jesus] by the Majestic Glory" (v. 17), Peter emphasized an even more certain and reliable place where God speaks: "We have something more sure, the prophetic word" (v. 19). *Note:* the ESV translation of this verse is good, but the NIV and NASB miss the point. With these words, Peter is emphasizing that the written Word of God is a greater source of certainty even than the transfiguration of our Lord, when God the Father spoke directly from heaven!

No One Has a Better Faith Than You Do!

Does strength of faith sometimes increase or decrease, or do some people have greater faith than others? See Matthew 8:5–13, 23–27. Jesus commended people for great faith (Matthew 8:10) and rebuked others for weak, or little, faith (v. 26). In any Christian, faith can be strong one moment and weak the next. Just think of the example of Peter, who first swore to remain faithful to Jesus and never deny Him, even in death (Matthew 26:33–35), but who then ran away from Jesus (v. 56) and denied knowing Him (vv. 69–75). If such swings in the strength of faith are possible for Peter, then they are certainly also possible for you and for me!

According to the following verses, who gives you the faith that you have?
Romans 10:17—Faith miraculously comes to you through hearing Jesus' words
Romans 12:3—God measures faith out to each Christian, some in larger amounts

than others, but "each according to the measure of faith that God has assigned."

Ephesians 2:8—Faith is not of yourself. It is the gift of God!

Despite your faith's strength or weakness in any given moment, what does Peter say about it in 2 Peter 1:1? Peter, a pillar of the Church and a favored disciple of our Lord, writes his letter "to those who have obtained a faith of equal standing with ours." That is to say, God's gift of faith to you places you on an equal plane and a level playing field with Peter and with all the other apostles. Theirs is not a superior faith or a more excellent spirituality! Theirs is "of equal standing" with yours and yours with theirs.

In what way does 2 Peter 1:1 give you a strong help against Pentecostals and other Gnostics? Gnostic and Pentecostal spirituality is essentially hierarchical. That is to say, there is always someone who claims to have more of the Spirit and the Spirit's gifts than you do. You might be a Christian, but just not yet as filled with the Spirit as the other guy. Peter throws a fireball at such claims! Your faith—the faith God gave to you at your infant Baptism—is of equal standing with the faith of Peter himself!

Despite what the Pentecostals and other Gnostics say, how can you be certain that you personally have the gift of the Holy Spirit? There are many ways to know that you personally have the Spirit. Here are just a few: First, are you baptized? If you are, then you have the Spirit, because Paul calls Baptism "the washing of regeneration and renewal of the Holy Spirit" (Titus 3:5). Second, do you believe what you hear and read in God's Bible? If you do, then you have the Spirit, because the Scriptures "are spiritually discerned" (1 Corinthians 2:14). Finally, do you believe and confess that Jesus is Lord? Good! "No one can say 'Jesus is Lord' except in the Holy Spirit" (1 Corinthians 12:3).

Closing Prayer

Heavenly Father, keep me firm in faith, now and always! By the power of Your Word and Spirit, teach me to focus my attention where You wish for Your voice to be heard—in Your Word and in Your Sacraments—and guard me always against all other voices, which only pose and masquerade as Your voice. Amen.

9

Gnostics

A Message from Martin Luther

Different spirits come along . . . and claim that they are the ones who have the Spirit. Their one boast is of nothing but the Spirit. And they bring some fine and alluring arguments and attractive words, as the Anabaptists and their ilk do today, and in years past the Montanists and many others did. Our whole quarrel with all these factions revolves about their claim that they have the Holy Spirit and that therefore they should be believed. (Luther's Works, American Edition, Volume 24, pages 176–77)

Opening Prayer

L: Long ago, at many times and in many ways, God spoke to our fathers by the prophets,

P: But in these last days He has spoken to us by His Son. (Hebrews 1:1–2a)

L: Do not add to His words,

P: Lest He rebuke you and you be found a liar. (Proverbs 30:6)

L: Forever, O LORD, Your word is firmly fixed in the heavens.

P: Your faithfulness endures to all generations. (Psalm 119:89–90a)

All Is Said That Shall Be Said

What does **Hebrews 1:1–2** say about the way God desires to speak to us, especially now that Jesus was born, suffered, died, and rose again?

Many theologians and Bible scholars note that some of the apostle John's writings were directed against early Gnostics. What warning does John speak in **Revelation 22:18–19?**

According to **Deuteronomy 4:2**; **12:32**; and **Proverbs 30:6**, is John's warning in **Revelation 22:18–19** a new idea?

The Lutheran reformers said, "God does not want to deal with us in any other way than through the spoken Word and the Sacraments" (Smalcald Articles, Part III, Article VIII, paragraph 10). Why is it so absolutely essential for you that God confine Himself to speaking *only* through His Word and Sacraments?

What does Peter emphasize in the last portion of **2 Peter 1:16–19**?

No One Has a Better Faith Than You Do!

Does strength of faith sometimes increase or decrease, or do some people have greater faith than others? See **Matthew 8:5–13, 23–27**.

According to the following verses, who gives you the faith that you have?

Romans 10:17

Romans 12:3

Ephesians 2:8

Despite your faith's strength or weakness in any given moment, what does Peter say about it in **2 Peter 1:1**?

In what way does **2 Peter 1:1** give you a strong help against Pentecostals and other Gnostics?

Despite what the Pentecostals and other Gnostics say, how can you be certain that you personally have the gift of the Holy Spirit?

10

Judaizers

Lesson Focus

God's apostle Paul opposed the Judaizers because they taught that in order to become a Christian, you must first become a Jew through circumcision. This teaching tempts you to believe that there are certain requirements that first must be met before you can be saved.

Historical Context

Most of the earliest Christians were Jewish converts. As the Gospel spread to the Gentiles, some of these Jewish Christians attempted to impose the Jewish way of life upon the Gentile converts. Various difficulties subsequently arose. For example, "When the disciples were increasing in number, a complaint by the Hellenists [Greeks] arose against the Hebrews because their widows were being neglected in the daily distribution" (Acts 6:1).

The big question was circumcision: must a Gentile observe this Jewish rite in order to become a Christian? The Judaizers emphatically answered YES! The Letter to the Galatians is the apostle Paul's thundering NO!

This question placed Peter and Paul at odds for a while (Galatians 2). Peter had been associating with Gentile Christians, accepting them as brothers in every way, until some of his Jewish friends came to visit. Then, in order to meet the expectations of these friends, Peter distanced himself from his Gentile brothers. Paul called Peter to account, and Peter repented of this false teaching and loveless practice.

Jewish ceremonial law remains a tantalizing temptation for many Christians today. For example, while circumcision is no longer a major issue, many Christians participate in reenactments of the old Jewish festivals, especially the Passover Seder. Christians should be careful! Passover ceremonies anticipated the coming of Christ. When practiced today, these ceremonies may constitute a denial of the Christ who has come.

Distribute copies of Participant Page 10 if desired. Read aloud the Historical Context, above, and the Message from Martin Luther. Then pray responsively the Opening Prayer.

A Message from Martin Luther

I hear that in Austria and Moravia some Judaizers are today advocating both the Sabbath and circumcision. If they were to move against those who are not fortified beforehand by the Word of God, they would surely cause much harm. (Luther's Works, American Edition, Volume 3, page 77)

Opening Prayer

L: I went down to the land whose bars closed upon me forever;

P: Yet You brought up my life from the pit, O LORD my God. (Jonah 2:6b)

L: O LORD, You have brought up my soul from Sheol;

P: You restored me to life from among those who go down to the pit.
(Psalm 30:3)

L: Forever, O LORD, Your word is firmly fixed in the heavens.

P: Your faithfulness endures to all generations. (Psalm 119:89–90a)

Old Testament Rites: Timothy and Titus

Paul allowed Timothy to be circumcised, but he refused the same for Titus. Why was this, according to Acts 16:1–3 and Galatians 2:3–5? Paul circumcised Timothy in order to remove a stumbling block for the Jews who had not yet heard the Gospel of Christ. Paul did not want these Jews immediately to raise objections to what Paul was saying simply because Timothy was uncircumcised. Timothy's circumcision was not a matter of giving in to demands, but a matter of love.

In Titus's case, love demanded that he not be circumcised. Paul had begun to preach to the Gentiles, and Titus had joined him. When these two men, along with Barnabas, visited the apostles in Jerusalem, Titus was welcomed. It was "false brothers" (Galatians 2:4) who tried to insist on Titus's circumcision—"to them we did not yield in submission even for a moment" (v. 5), in order that the Gospel of Christ not have any conditions or prerequisites attached to it.

The Judaizers had been teaching that the Gospel of Jesus comes with the precondition of circumcision. What does Paul call this "gospel" in Galatians 1:6–9? A gospel that comes with a precondition or prerequisite is "a different gospel . . . a gospel contrary to the one we [Paul] preached." The NIV wording is helpful: "a different gospel—which is really no gospel at all" (vv. 6–7).

Why is this topic so important, according to Galatians 2:15–21 and 3:10? As soon as any precondition or prerequisite is added to the Gospel about Jesus, the message stops being about Jesus and starts being about what you must do. Such a message is not Gospel, but Law! However, even Jews in Paul's day knew that "a person is not justified by works of the law but through faith in Jesus Christ" (2:15). Why? Because "all who rely on works of the law are under a curse" (3:10). This, in fact, is the message of the Old Testament, which is why Paul cited Deuteronomy 27:26.

About what does Paul speak in Galatians 5:1–6? Paul speaks about the freedom that is now ours in Christ. This is not a freedom to live in reckless abandon or uninhibited sin, but freedom from the bondage of the Law. This freedom means that there are no prerequisites to your salvation. Jesus has done all for you, has given all for you, and will complete all for you. Not even faith is something that you must provide! Jesus gives you His gift of faith by the miraculous power of the Good News that has been preached to you (Romans 10:17).

Old Testament Rites: John's Baptism

What miraculous gift did the Baptism of John the Baptist bestow, according to Luke 3:3? John's Baptism gave God's miraculous gift of forgiveness to those who received it. John was "proclaiming a baptism of repentance *for* the forgiveness of sins" (Luke 3:3, emphasis added). In its Old Testament, precrucifixion context, John's Baptism provided all the miraculous gifts from God that your New Testament Baptism provides for you today!

What had happened—it is the single most important event in all of human history—between the time John baptized in the Jordan and the conversation Paul had in Corinth, Acts 19:1–5? By the time the men in Corinth had received John's Baptism, Jesus had already died, resurrected, and ascended into heaven. Because John's Baptism was an Old Testament Baptism that looked forward to the cross, the crucifixion fulfilled, completed, and rendered obsolete John's Baptism. The postcrucifixion Baptism is Baptism in the name of Jesus (Acts 2:38); or, stated in a more detailed way, "in the name of the Father and of the Son and of the Holy Spirit" (Matthew 28:19).

Here is an analogy to help you understand how Jesus' crucifixion changed the meaning of John's Baptism from sacrament to empty rite. In 1982, a pop artist named Prince released a song titled "1999." The main lyric was, "Tonight I'm gonna party like it's 1999." Back in 1982, this song evoked a feeling of reckless, end-of-time abandon. Its lyric was similar to saying, "Tonight I am going to party like there is no tomorrow." More than a decade later, the song "1999" no longer carried a sense of future, end-time recklessness. Today it carries a sense of nostalgia—memories of yesteryear—for those who remember it. What happened? The year 1999 came and went, and when it did, the meaning of the song changed forever.

In a similar way, John's Baptism for the forgiveness of sins looked forward to the coming of Christ. When the death and resurrection of Christ passed, the meaning of John's Baptism changed forever. His Baptism no longer had anything toward which to look. It became an empty rite. That is why Paul baptized the men in Corinth who had only received John's Baptism. Paul gave them God's New Testament Sacrament of forgiveness!

How might Paul's rejection of John's Baptism shape your view toward the other Old Testament rites, such as Passover Seders, which many Christians find appealing today? John's Baptism was more than useless after the death and resurrection of Jesus. John's Baptism was potentially dangerous to those who received it! If the men in Corinth had clung to John's Baptism, refusing the New Testament Baptism Paul wanted to give, they would have been denying Christ. By clinging to John's Baptism, these men essentially would have been saying, "We are still waiting and still looking forward to the coming of Messiah." This, of course, would have been a denial of Jesus, the Messiah, who had already come.

Similar dangers attach themselves to Christian reenactments of Passover Seders today, and Christians should view such reenactments warily. This author believes such reenactments are a particularly bad idea, because the rites of the Old Testament were all fulfilled and rendered obsolete with the coming of Christ. This author realizes that many Christians feel attracted to reenactments of Old Testament rites as a way of understanding—but I also believe some things do not need to be understood. Do we need to kill a lamb and a bull, too, in order to understand the Old Testament sacrificial system? For that matter, what benefit would this act give to our faith? Faith comes by hearing the Word of Christ (Romans 10:17), not by reenacting Jewish life. The old ways, which looked forward to Christ, should be put away forever now that Christ has come (Luke 5:38–39).

Out with the Old!

According to Colossians 2:9–12, what new act has replaced the Old Testament act of circumcision? Baptism is "a circumcision made without hands" (v. 11). It is the miracle that joins you to the perfect, once-for-all "circumcision of Christ, having been buried with Him in baptism" (vv. 11–12).

Does this mean male Christian babies should never be circumcised? Some Christians might elect to circumcise their sons for other reasons: health, family tradition, and so forth. The act itself is not forbidden, as shown by Timothy's circumcision. It is the obligation of circumcision, required by the Judaizers, that destroys faith in Christ.

What meal does Jesus give in Matthew 26:26–29 to replace the Old Testament rite of Passover? What does Jesus especially promise you in verse 29? Just as New Testament Baptism has replaced circumcision (Colossians 2:9–12), Holy Communion has likewise replaced the Passover meal. In Holy Communion, Jesus promises to be with you, eating and drinking with you in the Father's kingdom, which came to you and was established for you in Jesus' incarnation, death, and resurrection.

Closing Prayer

Thank You, Jesus, that You have done all things for me and for my salvation. By the power of Your Word and Spirit, continually draw me to those New Testament gifts You have given, which assure me that all has been fully accomplished. Amen.

10

A Message from Martin Luther

I hear that in Austria and Moravia some Judaizers are today advocating both the Sabbath and circumcision. If they were to move against those who are not fortified beforehand by the Word of God, they would surely cause much harm. (Luther's Works, American Edition, Volume 3, page 77)

Opening Prayer

L: I went down to the land whose bars closed upon me forever;

P: Yet You brought up my life from the pit, O Lord my God. (Jonah 2:6b)

L: O Lord, You have brought up my soul from Sheol;

P: You restored me to life from among those who go down to the pit. (Psalm 30:3)

L: Forever, O Lord, Your word is firmly fixed in the heavens.

P: Your faithfulness endures to all generations. (Psalm 119:89–90a)

Old Testament Rites: Timothy and Titus

Paul allowed Timothy to be circumcised, but he refused the same for Titus. Why was this, according to **Acts 16:1–3** and **Galatians 2:3–5**?

The Judaizers had been teaching that the Gospel of Jesus comes with the precondition of circumcision. What does Paul call this "gospel" in **Galatians 1:6–9**?

Why is this topic so important, according to **Galatians 2:15–21** and **3:10**?

About what does Paul speak in **Galatians 5:1–6**?

Old Testament Rites: John's Baptism

What miraculous gift did the Baptism of John the Baptist bestow, according to **Luke 3:3**?

What had happened—it is the single most important event in all of human history—between the time John baptized in the Jordan and the conversation Paul had in Corinth, **Acts 19:1–5**?

How might Paul's rejection of John's Baptism shape your view toward the other Old Testament rites, such as Passover Seders, which many Christians find appealing today?

Out with the Old!

According to **Colossians 2:9–12**, what new act has replaced the Old Testament act of circumcision?

Does this mean male Christian babies should never be circumcised?

What meal does Jesus give in **Matthew 26:26–29** to replace the Old Testament rite of Passover? What does Jesus especially promise you in **verse 29**?

11

Pelagians

Lesson Focus

Pelagius taught that humanity was damaged by Adam and Eve's fall into sin, but it was not totally and entirely corrupted; a remnant of free will remained. This teaching will tempt you to think that you have something good inside of you to offer Jesus, such as your love, your faith, or your cooperation in salvation.

Historical Context

Pelagius was an early-fifth-century theologian who held that it was not entirely necessary to rely upon the grace of Christ for salvation. Enough goodness remained in humanity to make it possible for a person to do good works and gain God's favor. All a person needed to do was to develop his or her inborn morality to a level that God finds acceptable. Because the notion of salvation apart from Christ defies the very essence of Christianity, Pelagius and his followers were condemned by the Council of Ephesus in 431 AD.

A modified form of Pelagius's teaching, called Semi-Pelagianism, has persisted through the centuries and can be found still today. While Semi-Pelagians reject the Pelagian idea that salvation can be obtained apart from Christ, they do not deny the freedom of the will. Semi-Pelagians insist that the individual human must cooperate with—or at least agree with—God in order to receive salvation. If you want to hear an example of modern Semi-Pelagianism, simply tune in to a television preacher and listen to him explain how Jesus wants to save you, but you must first make your "personal decision" and ask Him into your heart.

Distribute copies of Participant Page 11 if desired. Read aloud the Historical Context, above, and the Message from the Lutheran Confessions. Then pray responsively the Opening Prayer.

A Message from the Lutheran Confessions

> We also reject the error of the Semi-Pelagians. They teach that a person by his own powers can begin his conversion, but cannot complete it without the Holy Spirit's grace. (Epitome of the Formula of Concord, Article II, paragraph 10)

Opening Prayer

L: May all who seek You rejoice and be glad in You!

P: May those who love Your salvation say evermore, "God is great!"

L: But I am poor and needy; hasten to me, O God!

P: You are my help and my deliverer; O Lord, do not delay! (Psalm 70:4–5)

L: Forever, O Lord, Your word is firmly fixed in the heavens.

P: Your faithfulness endures to all generations. (Psalm 119:89–90a)

The Bondage of the Will

In these following verses, what key words describe our condition as a result of our sin?

Ephesians 2:1, 5—Paul says that we were dead in sin and trespasses. Dead people can do nothing to help themselves!

Romans 7:18—Contrary to the Pelagian claim, Paul confesses, "I know that nothing good dwells in me, that is, in my flesh."

1 Corinthians 2:14—Unaided by God Himself, the Scriptures do not even make sense to "the natural person," that is, to the person born with the disease of sin and death.

Job 15:14–16—Humankind is so inwardly corrupt that God absolutely refuses to trust humanity to do anything well.

Return to Ephesians 2:1, 5. How does Paul describe God's salvation in keeping with his description of our sin? Salvation is nothing less than a resurrection from the dead! We were dead in trespasses and sins, but God makes us alive in Christ. Because salvation is a resurrection from the dead, no person can claim to play a role, no matter how small, in it.

Think of Lazarus as an example (John 11:38–44). Was Lazarus able to exercise his will or "make a personal decision for Jesus"? Lazarus had no power except for the power of Jesus' words. In the same way that Lazarus awoke from the dead by the power of the Word, those who are dead in trespasses and sins (Ephesians 2:1) likewise believe solely by the power of the Word. There is no exercise of the will in becoming Christian; there is only the miraculous gift of faith, given to you by God.

Through the Power of the Word

By what means does God the Holy Spirit raise you from the death of your sins?

Romans 1:16—God uses the Gospel, "the power of God for salvation," to raise you from the death of your sins.

Romans 10:17—God uses the miracle of faith, which comes by hearing the words of Christ, to raise you from the death of your sins.

1 Corinthians 3:5–7—Salvation takes place when God causes the growth. No one can claim credit for his or her own salvation, or for the salvation of others. Suppose you tell your friend about Jesus and invite him or her to church. Subsequently, your friend desires to be baptized into the faith. Does this mean that you made a Christian? No! God makes Christians through your planting and watering—He alone gets the credit for the growth.

Why is it so essential that God be the only one who contributes to our salvation, without any contribution from us? The moment a Christian begins to feel as though he or she possesses something inwardly good apart from Christ, that is the moment that trust in Christ begins to wane. This is why C. F. W. Walther, the first president of the Lutheran Church-Missouri Synod, wrote: "A preacher of the Law must make a person distrust himself even in the least matter until his dying hour and keep him confessing that he is a miserable creature, with no record of good deeds except those which God has accomplished through him" (*The Proper Distinction Between Law and Gospel*, page 134).

The Persistence of the Sinful Flesh

What complaint does Paul speak in Romans 7:15–20? Paul complains that, even as a Christian, he cannot do any of the good that he wishes to do. He always has good intentions, but sin always gets in the way, and things do not work out the way Paul desires.

Have you also experienced a similar conflict? Answers, of course, will vary. This is a good time to discuss how Paul's struggle in Romans 7:15–20 is not his alone, but it is the struggle of every Christian who ever lived.

In what way is it a benefit and blessing to you that you will never be able to master the Ten Commandments and stop sinning, so long as you remain in this life? If any of us were to master the Ten Commandments and stop sinning, we would immediately forget about Christ and stop trusting in Him. One of the blessings of our ongoing struggle with sin is that this struggle continually chases us back to Jesus, to His forgiveness, and to the new life He promises us.

Closing Prayer

O God, You alone are the strength and source of my faith. By the power of Your Word and Spirit, never allow me to trust in my own strength or power, but teach me to trust only in the merits of my Lord Jesus Christ, who has done all things for me and for my salvation. Amen.

11

A Message from the Lutheran Confessions

We also reject the error of the Semi-Pelagians. They teach that a person by his own powers can begin his conversion, but cannot complete it without the Holy Spirit's grace. (Epitome of the Formula of Concord, Article II, paragraph 10)

Opening Prayer

L: May all who seek You rejoice and be glad in You!

P: May those who love Your salvation say evermore, "God is great!"

L: But I am poor and needy; hasten to me, O God!

P: You are my help and my deliverer; O LORD, do not delay!
(Psalm 70:4–5)

L: Forever, O LORD, Your word is firmly fixed in the heavens.

P: Your faithfulness endures to all generations.
(Psalm 119:89–90a)

The Bondage of the Will

In these following verses, what key words describe our condition as a result of our sin?

Ephesians 2:1, 5

Romans 7:18

1 Corinthians 2:14

Job 15:14–16

Return to **Ephesians 2:1, 5**. How does Paul describe God's salvation in keeping with his description of our sin?

Think of Lazarus as an example (**John 11:38–44**). Was Lazarus able to exercise his will or "make a personal decision for Jesus"?

Through the Power of the Word

By what means does God the Holy Spirit raise you from the death of your sins?

Romans 1:16

Romans 10:17

1 Corinthians 3:5–7

Why is it so essential that God be the only one who contributes to our salvation, without any contribution from us?

The Persistence of the Sinful Flesh

What complaint does Paul speak in **Romans 7:15–20**?

Have you also experienced a similar conflict?

In what way is it a benefit and blessing to you that you will never be able to master the Ten Commandments and stop sinning, so long as you remain in this life?

12

Sadducees and Corinthians

Lesson Focus

If there is no resurrection of the dead, then not even Christ has been raised. And if Christ has not been raised, then our preaching is in vain and your faith is in vain. . . . Your faith is futile and you are still in your sins. (1 Corinthians 15:13–14, 17)

Historical Context

The Sadducees were a Jewish sect, prominent in Jesus' day, which believed there was no resurrection from the dead. The ancient historian Josephus explained that the Sadducees' overarching belief was that the soul dies with the body (*Antiquities* 18 1 4). Because of this assumption, the Sadducees refused to listen to many passages of the Old Testament that speak about the resurrection and eternal life. This is why Jesus said the Sadducees knew "neither the Scriptures nor the power of God" (Matthew 22:29).

The ancient Greeks (including the Corinthians) shared the Sadducees' disbelief in the resurrection, but for different reasons. Neoplatonic dualism (Lesson 3) held that only spiritual things are good; all physical things are evil. Salvation meant escape from the body. Why would anyone want to have his or her physical body resurrected after he or she has died? This rejection of the resurrection led to Paul's famous treatise on the resurrection in 1 Corinthians 15.

Many people today call themselves Christians but also deny every miraculous aspect of the faith. This is especially true among Christians who say the Bible is not God's Word, or the Bible only *contains* God's Word. Such people say the miracles recorded in the Bible are nothing more than human stories, dreamed up for the sake of teaching the faith. They believe Christianity is only about the way we live in this life, and there is no resurrection from the dead. Paul's judgment, stated in the Lesson Focus, above, is for them.

Distribute copies of Participant Page 12 if desired. Read aloud the Historical Context, above, and the Message from Martin Luther. Then pray responsively the Opening Prayer.

A Message from Martin Luther

The Sadducees and the Epicureans [Greek philosophers] maintain that God is the God of the dead. Christ, on the other hand, teaches (Matt. 22:32) that God is the God of the living. (Luther's Works, American Edition, Volume 3, page 118)

There are still many who do not believe this [the resurrection of Christ] in their hearts and secretly regard this as a big laugh, especially those who claim to be smart and very intelligent and who measure and judge God's Word with their reason. They are like the Sadducees and their disciples in the days of Christ, who spread that poison among God's people. (Luther's Works, American Edition, Volume 28, page 100)

Opening Prayer

L: After my skin has been thus destroyed, yet in my flesh I shall see God,

P: Whom I shall see for myself,

L: And my eyes shall behold, and not another.

P: My heart faints within me! (Job 19:26–27)

L: Forever, O Lord, Your word is firmly fixed in the heavens.

P: Your faithfulness endures to all generations. (Psalm 119:89–90a)

The Old Testament Hope of Resurrection

What do the following verses teach you about the hope and certainty of God's Old Testament Christians concerning resurrection of the dead?

Job 19:25–27—Job confidently confessed that he would be raised from the dead and given back his own, personal body. Job believed that he would see God with his own eyes, even after his flesh had been destroyed by the decay of death. Every aspect of Job's faith yearned for the resurrection, expressed by his words "My heart faints within me!" (v. 27).

Jonah 2:1–10—In a manner that prefigured Jesus' own death (Matthew 12:38–40), Jonah gave himself up for dead while he was in the belly of the great fish. Yet Jonah did not lose hope! Jonah's certainty of the resurrection is expressed several times here, including these phrases: "I shall again look upon Your holy temple" (Jonah 2:4); "You brought up

my life from the pit" (v. 6); and "I with the voice of thanksgiving will sacrifice to You; what I have vowed I will pay" (v. 9).

Genesis 22:9–10 and Hebrews 11:17–19—Abraham raised his knife against his son, even though Isaac was to be the one through whom the Messiah comes, because Abraham "considered that God was able even to raise him [Isaac] from the dead" (Hebrews 11:19).

Was the resurrection of Jesus, the long-awaited Christ, likewise part of the Old Testament faith?

Psalm 16:7–10 and Acts 2:25–28—In his Pentecost sermon in Acts 2, Peter explained that the promise of resurrection in Psalm 16 is a promise spoken to Christ. With the exception of Christ, the bodies of all who die will decay. But God promised that Christ, His Holy One, would not decay.

Isaiah 53:10–12—In this most famous Old Testament prophecy concerning Christ, God the Father promises that His Son, His Suffering Servant, "shall see His offspring; He shall prolong His days" (v. 10). Because Christ poured out His life into death, God will "divide Him a portion with the many" (v. 12), that is, give Jesus an inheritance. Because only living people receive an inheritance, this verse prophesies Jesus' resurrection.

Jonah 2:10 and Matthew 12:38–40—While Jonah's song expressed his own personal hope and certainty of the resurrection, his words also speak prophetically about Christ's own certainty of the resurrection. Why? Because Jesus explains that "the sign of the prophet Jonah" (Matthew 12:39), that is, the vomiting out of Jonah by the fish, is a prophecy of Christ's resurrection in particular.

1 Corinthians 15

What do 1 Corinthians 1:18–21 and 2:16 say about human wisdom? Human wisdom amounts to nothing and is nothing more than foolishness in the eyes of God. Dualism was nothing more than an idea dreamed up by a philosopher whom other people thought was wise. But philosophy is foolishness in the eyes of God! Those who hear and believe in the resurrection do so by the power of the cross of Christ, which appears to be nothing but foolishness and waste in the eyes of the world.

According to 1 Corinthians 15:3–8, does the Christian faith rely upon human wisdom as a basis for its hope in the resurrection? No! The Christian faith does not rely upon human wisdom, but it relies upon the Good News that the prophets and apostles received from God. Paul, for example, merely passes on "as of first importance what I also received" (v. 3). Stated another way, Paul did not dream up the resurrection as if it were merely a human, philosophical idea. The resurrection is God's own revelation.

Dualism led many Corinthian Christians to think that the resurrection was not an important part of the Christian faith. How does Paul respond in 1 Corinthians 15:12–19? If the resurrection is not part of the faith, then Christ did not rise. If Christ did not rise, then there is no point to your faith! "Our preaching is in vain and your faith is in vain" (v. 14). Those who believe that the Christian faith is mostly about the way we live our lives here on earth are to be pitied more than all others.

In 1 Corinthians 15:35–49, how does Paul help you think about what the resurrection body will look like? Paul uses the analogy of a seed, which is a very helpful way of thinking about the resurrection body. Suppose you examine the seed of a plant, but you do not know what sort of seed it is. The only way to find out is to plant the seed and watch it grow. Even so, all of that "future plant" is already contained in the seed.

In the same way, says Paul, your human body is like a seed. When it is "planted" in death, you cannot yet tell how the resurrection body will look. Yet it will be the same body that was planted! Your body now "contains" your resurrection body, so to speak, in the same way that a seed contains a future plant.

More Than Going to Heaven!

When a Christian dies, many people comfort themselves by saying, "This person has gone to heaven." In what way is the promise of the resurrection an even stronger consolation for mourning? Far from merely going to a spiritual life in heaven, the resurrection promises your body back to you! Unencumbered by the weight of sin and death, your new resurrection body will be imperishable and perfect in every way. You will in your body live with Christ eternally!

What harsh warning does the resurrection speak to all unbelievers? See Isaiah 66:24 and Matthew 10:28. In the same way that believers will rise, so also will all unbelievers. However, unbelievers rise not to eternal life, but to eternal torment and death, where "their worm shall not die, their fire shall not be quenched, and they shall be an abhorrence to all flesh" (Isaiah 66:24). This is why Jesus warns His Christians not to fear those who can harm only the body. Such enemies can only harm the physical body, but they have no power over the resurrection to eternal life. Rather, the One to be feared is He who can destroy both soul and body in hell.

What comfort does Paul give in 1 Thessalonians 4:13–18? In the resurrection of all flesh, there will be a great reunion of those who die in the Christian faith. "The dead in Christ will rise first" (v. 16), but we will not be left behind! We, too, will rise, and as one eternal family, we will "meet the Lord in the air" (v. 17).

Closing Prayer

Because You live, Jesus, I also shall live; because You have risen from the dead, I, too, shall rise. By the power of Your Word and Spirit, keep the hope and promise of the resurrection firmly planted in my heart and mind, as this hope provides endurance in all hardship. Amen.

12

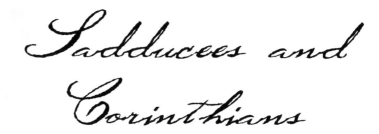

Sadducees and Corinthians

A Message from Martin Luther

The Sadducees and the Epicureans [Greek philosophers] maintain that God is the God of the dead. Christ, on the other hand, teaches (Matt. 22:32) that God is the God of the living. (Luther's Works, American Edition, Volume 3, page 118)

There are still many who do not believe this [the resurrection of Christ] in their hearts and secretly regard this as a big laugh, especially those who claim to be smart and very intelligent and who measure and judge God's Word with their reason. They are like the Sadducees and their disciples in the days of Christ, who spread that poison among God's people. (Luther's Works, American Edition, Volume 28, page 100)

Opening Prayer

L: After my skin has been thus destroyed, yet in my flesh I shall see God,

P: Whom I shall see for myself,

L: And my eyes shall behold, and not another.

P: My heart faints within me! (Job 19:26–27)

L: Forever, O Lord, Your word is firmly fixed in the heavens.

P: Your faithfulness endures to all generations. (Psalm 119:89–90a)

The Old Testament Hope of Resurrection

What do the following verses teach you about the hope and certainty of God's Old Testament Christians concerning resurrection of the dead?

Job 19:25–27

Jonah 2:1–10

Genesis 22:9–10 and **Hebrews 11:17–19**

Was the resurrection of Jesus, the long-awaited Christ, likewise part of the Old Testament faith?

Psalm 16:7–10 and **Acts 2:25–28**

Isaiah 53:10–12

Jonah 2:10 and **Matthew 12:38–40**

1 Corinthians 15

What do **1 Corinthians 1:18–21** and **2:16** say about human wisdom?

According to **1 Corinthians 15:3–8**, does the Christian faith rely upon human wisdom as a basis for its hope in the resurrection?

Dualism led many Corinthian Christians to think that the resurrection was not an important part of the Christian faith. How does Paul respond in **1 Corinthians 15:12–19**?

In **1 Corinthians 15:35–49**, how does Paul help you think about what the resurrection body will look like?

More Than Going to Heaven!

When a Christian dies, many people comfort themselves by saying, "This person has gone to heaven." In what way is the promise of the resurrection an even stronger consolation for mourning?

What harsh warning does the resurrection speak to all unbelievers? See **Isaiah 66:24** and **Matthew 10:28**.

What comfort does Paul give in **1 Thessalonians 4:13–18**?

Photo Credits